LIBERAL MISERY

HOW THE HATEFUL LEFT SUCKS JOY OUT OF EVERYTHING AND EVERYONE

EDDIE SCARRY

Published by Bombardier Books
An Imprint of Post Hill Press
ISBN: 978-1-63758-435-4
ISBN (eBook): 978-1-63758-436-1

Liberal Misery:
How the Hateful Left Sucks Joy Out of Everything and Everyone

Cover Design by Matt Margolis

Post Hill Press
New York • Nashville
posthillpress.com

Published in the United States of America
1 2 3 4 5 6 7 8 9 10

Also by Eddie Scarry

Privileged Victims: How America's Culture Fascists Hijacked the Country and Elevated Its Worst People

For every liberal who ruined anyone's day with their self-entitlement and grotesque behavior. Go fuck yourselves.

Contents

Introduction: Dear, Sweet Liberals: Show Us on the Doll Where He Touched You ix

1: Democrats: Can't Live With 'Em, Can't Live Without 'Em Ruining Everything.... 1

2: The Left Loved the Pandemic and They Wanted You to Love It, Too 13

3: Spot the White Supremacist (Hint: He's Black) 59

4: "Insurrection," American White Nationalism, and Other Urban Legends of the Toxic Left 85

5: Thou Shalt Not Speak Unless Truly Boring.... 113

Conclusion: Learning to Live with Liberals, Rule #1: Don't Feed the Animals 125

Acknowledgments 129

About the Author.... 131

INTRODUCTION

Dear, Sweet Liberals: Show Us on the Doll Where He Touched You

It made some sense that liberal Democrats would be bitter immediately after the 2016 election. The country had just denied Hillary Clinton—yes, Empress Hillary Clinton—as heir to her throne and instead chose to elevate a foul-mouthed barbarian named Donald Trump to the presidency. He liked eating meatloaf and well-done steaks. Ew!

A true outsider who represented all the things liberals hate—masculinity, optimism, independence—ruined the illusion that America was now exclusively their domain, a place they had hoped to use for their racial fixations, "green energy" projects, and weird gender-bender social experiments.

They lost. And losing hurts. But it's not supposed to be permanent. The next critical election is always within arm's reach and there are more productive ways to spend time than holding on to the pain of the last one.

As of 2016, though, liberals and Democrats no longer saw things that way, if they ever truly did at all. After that election, they saw no reason to pretend that they understood differences of political opinion nor that they could tolerate them. They no longer viewed Republicans, conservatives, or even just open-minded independents as the opposition in an honest democracy. They saw them all as an existential enemy that needed to be extinguished.

And thus began our long journey through hell. Pussy hats. Public crying. Fake hate crimes perpetrated by nonexistent Trump supporters. Safe spaces. Angry, vulgar protests broadcast on network television under the guise of being Hollywood award ceremonies. The tragic rise of liberal "civil rights attorney" Ben Crump. On and on.

And if you thought the four years under Trump were bad, those were a piece of cake compared with what would come. A presidential election was approaching and the economy was booming. What were Democrats and their reliable friends in the news media left to do other than turn up the dial to a breaking point, generate mass hysteria, and promise the public that it would only go away if they were put in charge?

A mysterious virus, violent rioting, and an all-around bitchy, insufferable atmosphere imposed on us by half of the country was just the ticket in 2020, it seemed. All of it was amplified by the media. All of it appears to have worked well to scare the living shit out of innocent and unassuming voters. And all of it provided the Left with a veil of sanctimony, a way for liberals to say, "Do as we tell you and the noise and chaos will go away. This is Trump's fault and if it weren't for him being president, we wouldn't be here."

It was fraudulent but enough reasonable voters found it persuasive. The bigger problem, however, was that by validating the tactic—the manufactured misery—Americans effectively encouraged the Left's worst impulse, which is to spread its own bitterness, joylessness, and misery.

Think about it. Even when liberal Democrats emerged victorious from the suffocating bonfire of 2020 and then had control of the White House and all of Congress for two years, did their mood change? No. It only got worse.

They may have traded their pussy hats for Fauci prayer candles but the attitude has never been angrier or more spiteful. Vengeance has animated them each and every day.

There are scores of studies, surveys, reports and data to back it up, but, like others, I also know it so well firsthand.

Back in November 2021 I was sitting with two friends at the bar of All Purpose, a popular pizza restaurant in Washington, D.C. One friend, a white woman in her early 30s, had exchanged niceties with the bar server, also a white woman who appeared to be also in her 30s and with dyed hair that made it look like a mix between silver and very light purple.

My friends and I at one point were discussing the not-guilty verdict that had just been rendered in the trial of Kyle Rittenhouse. I mentioned that it was amazing how many people were under the impression that Rittenhouse was prosecuted for shooting blacks, when in fact all parties involved with his case were white. My friend said that nonetheless, she believed that racism colored the outcome of the trial.

"What makes it racist?" I asked.

Immediately, the bartender with the dye job looked up from the drink she was preparing to declare, "WHAT MAKES IT RACIST IS—"

But just as quick as she was to insert herself, I held up my hand with the palm facing her and said, "We were just talking among ourselves."

"Okay, no problem," she said. And then I watched her for the duration of our time sitting there as she walked around, alerting every other member of staff about the belligerent racist who wouldn't let her speak.

I mean, I don't know for certain that's what she was telling her coworkers but is there any doubt? That's precisely what a liberal would do, particularly in Washington, where they all believe it's their moral duty to thrust themselves into any situation they have an opinion on.

And the irony is that in the bartender's mind, despite her having been the one to pipe up, uninvited, in a conversation between paying customers she does not know, she believed I was the asshole. I would have been perfectly justified in arguing with her to the point of making her cry tears of rage (she totally would have) because it wasn't me who felt entitled to toss my opinion at a complete stranger. Instead, I reminded the server that I was engaging my friends in an exclusive conversation, not navigating an open internet chatroom.

This isn't normal behavior. Normal people don't assume it's their place to butt in on the discussions of strangers, let alone when those strangers are the ones who will be deciding how much of a tip to leave.

The level of discomfort that these monsters are willing to instill on well-meaning, unassuming people has no boundaries. It can be minor, say a cold shoulder at a social gathering, and it can be extreme to the point of obscenity.

I met my boyfriend at the end of summer 2021. He's a political centrist in every sense, which is rare in deeply liberal Washington, D.C., particularly among the city's gays (who are perhaps the worst people on the planet, other than pedophiles and Rep. James Clyburn). After close to two years of traumatic dating (COVID and BLM 2020 turned up the temperature 1,000 degrees on how bitchy liberal gays could be), it was the freshest breath of air to meet someone who didn't want to slice my throat open for voicing an opinion he either didn't agree with or had never considered.

Living a virtually apolitical life had served him well. But then he met me. And when a certain friend circle of his found out who he was dating, being politically agnostic wasn't good enough for them. They expected him to take a stand—against me!

These were people I had not even met. They knew nothing about me personally and I knew nothing about them. But they had seen my work and TV appearances I shared on social media. That's all they needed to decide I wasn't worth knowing and that it was unacceptable for their friend to date me. I couldn't even be given the courtesy of meeting in person before knowing that I must be awful.

I had never experienced anything like it. I wasn't abusing my boyfriend. I didn't hit him. I didn't emotionally manipulate him. I didn't even talk about politics without him bringing it up first (which was often because, like a normal person, he was curious and had an open mind when talking about something with someone who just might know more about it than he does).

One person in particular had multiple interventions with my boyfriend. This person told him that "everyone" is going to think he's weird for seeing me, that the views I express are out of line, and that meeting me was not something he would ever be interested in doing.

Another gay liberal was out with my boyfriend one night and pulled up my Twitter profile and proceeded to go through my postings, reading them aloud, and declaring them unacceptable.

Who does this on a weekend night out? You might say I've written some controversial things but that only means that some people agree with it and some don't. We've gone from "agree to disagree" to "do not associate with the person who has a different opinion."

In saner parts of the country, friends celebrate when one of their own has found a match who makes him happy. That's not the case anymore with so many liberals. They now see it as necessary to make clear that they disapprove if that match runs afoul of their weird ideology.

It can't be emphasized enough that this was a situation where people I had never met actively hated me and actively hated that their friend was happy with someone they did not want to know.

It's sick. There's no other word for it. But this is now the standard. They're angry and they want you to know it. Without having met you, they know they don't like you. And they will make sure you know it, too.

A critic might consider that these are one-offs, chance encounters, anecdotal, or cherry-pickings. They're not. They're exactly what right-leaning and independent Americans are experiencing every day, usually by complete surprise. It shouldn't be a surprise anymore.

The "Libs of Tik Tok" Twitter account was wildly popular for documenting and sharing these types of people, in their own words. Libs of Tik Tok simply re-posted the aggressive and bizarre musings of liberals who were sharing their views on social media. The transgender militants who wanted to explain the details of their sex mutation to children, the "queer" women who ranted about white men, and the blue-haired weirdos who desperately need the world to know how much they love and respect black people.

Libs of Tik Tok did nothing more than elevate publicly available social media posts to a wider audience so that more people could see for themselves just how gross the Left can be. For that, a liberal nag at the Washington Post named Taylor Lorenz set out to identify of the account's creator, who had hoped to remain anonymous. Lorenz in April 2022 wrote a lengthy article not addressing the content of what Libs of Tik Tok was doing, but telling Post readers who the person was behind the account and even linking to material that included the creator's address.

Both Lorenz and the people she felt the need to protect—everyone in the postings amplified by Libs of Tik Tok—are one and the same. They're not interested in arguing ideas. They're here to impose their beliefs and make your life miserable if you resist.

Democrats nominated Joe Biden, once a vivacious and even aggressive man, suddenly a mild-mannered geriatric, who promised that if elected president, he would "shut down the virus." And yet, just months into his term, the US saw the beginning of what would be the largest wave of new infections of the entire pandemic. A new variant of the coronavirus was born and the pathogen continued to spread at a steady pace, killing more people in 2021 than it did in the previous year, even though Biden had the benefit of not just one or two, but three proven vaccines to head off COVID. Before December of 2021 was over, the daily case counts had eclipsed even the worst of what we saw under Trump, which was an average of 251,232 per day.

By mid-January of the next year, under Biden, that number almost quadrupled.[1]

Normal person: That's weird. I thought Biden said he would—

Liberal: YOU SHUT YOUR DIRTY MOUTH! FOLLOW THE SCIENCE AND STAY HOME!

Like every other Democrat who ran for president in 2020, Biden literally launched his campaign in 2019 with a corny theme. His was that he would "restore the soul of America," a little number he said he came up with after seeing imagery from the 2017 Unite the Right rally in Charlottesville, Virginia, where the last remaining anti-Semites in the country had congregated.

In other words, fomenting racial unrest was on the agenda. But fear not, with Trump out and a Democrat in, our soul would be restored!

Biden was elected. Does America's collective spirit feel anew? Not exactly. To the contrary, liberals have only cranked up the temperature in hell. The race rioting continues. Calls from Black Lives Matter activists to "defund the police" persist. Democrats and liberals maintain that anything short of acquiescence on matters of race (i.e., white people don't get to have a say) merits yet more accusations.

Normal person: I know that black lives matter, but when it comes to shrinking the police force, I just—

Liberal: SILENCE, WHITIE! YOU'VE HAD YOUR TURN TO SPEAK AND NOW IT'S TIME FOR YOU TO CHECK YOUR PRIVILEGE AND VOTE FOR DEMOCRATS!

I don't have a crystal ball, but all indications are that this is our "new normal": coexisting with a Left that has lost all sense of joy. Or at least the pretense of ever having had it. They now not only choose to wake up each day in anger but to share it with the world. If you or anyone else takes exception with that, they believe you're the problem.

Their thoughts and feelings about politics are no longer a piece of their lives, but all-consuming. It's not without consequence. When

---

1 "Coronavirus in the U.S.: Latest Map and Case Count," *New York Times.* https://www.nytimes.com/interactive/2021/us/covid-cases.html.

half the country chooses to exist in a perpetual state of irritability, vindictiveness, and intolerance, we're all forced to share in the misery.

With a liberal in tow, there is no guarantee that it will be a good day. Quite the opposite. A liberal can ruin even the happiest occasion.

Have you ever had to be roommates with a complete bitch of a person? Thanks to the twenty-four-hour news cycle, that's what coexisting with these people has become—all the time.

There is plenty of life experience proving that Democrats and liberals never see a reason to hold back in unleashing their gloom, whether it be at a birthday party, a Christmas dinner, a baby shower, or even just a small gathering for Friday evening drinks. In those moments, nobody wants to talk seriously about politics. Nobody except liberal Democrats. They'll bring it up without a second's reservation.

If they have a point to make (they always do), it will be made. Sorry if it killed the mood (it always does).

Right-leaning people enter a social setting of mixed company and are dreaded of a political subject coming up for discussion. They know that if a liberal is present, saying nothing or, at most, holding back their real feelings, is best. Offending anyone is the last thing they want to do.

On the other hand, liberals and Democrats show up and invariably pop off with complete certainty that what they have to say on political affairs is shared by everyone in the room. And their attitude is that if it's not, F*** YOU!

It's hard to believe that there was once a time when politics was exclusively a matter of voting on Election Day and, maybe, some mildly uncomfortable conversation with relatives during the holidays. How cute that was. But it's no longer the case. Now, the Left has made everything about politics. Every TV show, every award ceremony, and every professional sporting event is pressured by the Left to also serve as platforms for messages about social justice, racial equity, gender equality, diversity, or some other nauseating cause. Every major company, every celebrity, every athlete, every singer, actor, and comedian feels the crushing weight of liberals demanding them to bend the knee (literally), raise a fist, and pledge allegiance to the fight against white supremacy, toxic masculinity, Right-wing nationalism, transphobia, and on and on.

They all know what a failure to comply means—public torture. Angry protests, aggressive social media campaigns, and raging editorials in the national papers and on cable news. Better that they simply go along to get along. Post the black square on Instagram. Blast out the supportive company statement in solidarity. Choreograph the press conference. It's so much easier that way.

But even as it's easier for celebrities and CEOs to get liberals off their backs, it means that no one ever gets a break from the hostility, conflict, and confrontation that all of it stokes. Watching the Oscars becomes less about glamor and more about gripe. Logging onto Facebook becomes less about connecting and more about arguing. Attending a football game is less about competition and more about contention.

The anger of liberals is everywhere and the irony is that the people who created this ugly cemetery of a world then accuse the people who complain about it of being divisive and controversial. You're simply supposed to go with their miserable flow and if you say a word about it, you're the problematic one. When the media bemoan how polarized and tribal our lives have become, that's their way of spreading the blame for a perpetually tense environment constructed entirely by the Left.

A Democrat would of course say, "What about Trump? The name-calling, the tweets." Yeah, Trump did name-call and he did tweet. But his election and widespread support among voters was a reaction to the stifling atmosphere established by the Left—the national media, the entertainment industry, and the Democratic Party. That fact is reflected in what one recent study called the "exhausted majority."

In 2018, scholars Stephen Hawkins, Daniel Yudkin, Miriam Juan-Torres, and Tim Dixon published the report "Hidden Tribes: A

Study of America's Polarized Landscape," in which eight thousand people were surveyed and then divided into seven distinctive groups according to political ideology. On the farthest Left were the progressive activists. On the Right, traditional conservatives and devoted conservatives. In the middle were traditional liberals, passive liberals, the politically disengaged, and moderates. The authors collectively referred to these middle groups, making up 67 percent of those surveyed, as "the exhausted majority."[2]

Though the exhausted majority was composed of political moderates on the Left, Right, and center, the authors said this group's views did not strictly conform to any ideology. Most crucial, though, is that they shared "a sense of fatigue with our polarized national conversation, a willingness to be flexible in their political viewpoints, and a lack of voice in the national conversation."

The overwhelming majority, 82 percent, said "political correctness" is a problem in America. Even among the traditional liberals and passive liberals groups, between 70 and 80 percent identified so-called political correctness as a problem. But among the more rigid and extreme progressive activist group (making up just 8 percent of those surveyed) only 30 percent said that political correctness is a problem.

"Political correctness" as a concept is, the authors note, "hard to define," but experience has shown it to be a real thing that people know when they see. The study included a quote from one twenty-eight-year-old North Carolina woman from the passive liberals group more or less capturing political correctness as a feeling that every utterance carries an absurd capacity to hurt a person's feelings or provoke anger. "I have liberal views, but I think political correctness has gone too far, absolutely," she said. "We have gotten to a point where everybody is offended by the smallest thing."

---

2 Hawkins, Stephen, Yudkin, Daniel et al., "Hidden Tribes: A Study of America's Polarized Landscape," More in Common, Oct. 2018. https://hiddentribes.us/media/qfpekz4g/hidden_tribes_report.pdf.

A thirty-year-old Indiana woman in the traditional liberals group said, "[W]e have become a society that is offended at everything. There is a lot in today's society that was never discussed before such as sexual orientation or gender fluidity that is kind of new and people don't know how to handle that...and it is not so much that they are intentionally being disrespectful or offensive...It's a combination of lack of knowledge and maybe oversensitivity."

A thirty-year-old woman from Arizona in the politically disengaged group said, "Why do we have this need in the US to call out people for appreciating a culture?...It's becoming ridiculous."

A forty-year-old male from Chicago in the moderates group said, "It's a good idea to try to respect other religions, cultures, and orientations. At the same time, I do feel like sometimes we have pushed it down people's throats to the point of nausea."

Authors of the study further observed, "On issues ranging from gender and Islam to race and immigration, at least 50 percent of Americans claim there is 'pressure to think a certain way.' Even among liberal groups, a significant percentage feels constrained." Islam was identified as the most sensitive subject, with 66 percent of Americans saying they don't feel that it's "acceptable" to voice their views on the matter.

Put this into the context of Trump's 2016 campaign, during which the arguably most controversial thing he said was during a rally in South Carolina in December of 2015. "Donald J. Trump is calling for a total and complete shutdown of Muslims entering the United States," he said, "until our country's representatives can figure out what the hell is going on."

So "controversial" was Trump's call for a ban on noncitizen Muslims that a YouGov poll published three months later found that more than half of Americans supported it. Among just independent voters, support was at an astounding 62 percent.[3]

This isn't so much connecting dots as it is seeing what's right in front of our face. The activist political Left has become a suffocating force in every part of American life, from entertainment, to academia, to athletics, to private companies and, most depressingly, to everyday social encounters. To them, everything is "I'm offended" or "It's not okay to say that" or "What gives you the right?" or "That hurt my feelings and you should apologize." And it's everywhere, all the time.

Lucian Gideon Conway, a psychology professor at the University of Montana, published his own research on Trump and political correctness in early 2018, concluding that "[W]e need to look beyond simple markers of ideology to understand the Trump phenomenon" and how his 2016 victory represented a "cultural revolt against political correctness."[4]

Conway wrote that the rise of Trump was largely fueled not by Right-wing politics or any ideology at all, but that "people don't like to be told that they can't say certain things, and Trump represents a say-anything voice." He came to that conclusion by gauging the way a sample of American voters viewed Trump and his opponent. Hillary Clinton was preferred by most voters at first glance, but when they were presented with a statement that suggested restricting their speech or their willingness to express their opinions, the gap between the preference for Trump and Clinton was eliminated. "Just by bringing communication restrictions to mind in a way that had nothing directly to do with the candidates at all," Conway said, "our sample

---

3 Moore, Peter. "Divide on Muslim neighborhood patrols but majority now back Muslim travel ban," YouGovAmerica, March 28, 2016. https://today.yougov.com/topics/politics/articles-reports/2016/03/28/divide-muslim-neighborhood-patrols.

4 Gideon Conway, Lucian. "How a cultural revolt against 'political correctness' helped launch Trump into the presidency," LSE Phelan US Centre, Feb. 28, 2018. https://blogs.lse.ac.uk/usappblog/2018/02/28/how-a-cultural-revolt-against-political-correctness-helped-launch-trump-into-the-presidency/.

went from supporting Clinton to the two candidates being in nearly a dead heat."

And with that, we can slam the door on attributing any of the current political anger, bitterness, and havoc wrought on the country by the Left to Trump. The evidence shows that we're not where we are, in any way, because of him. The reality is that he got to the White House in no small part because liberals made it so that the rest of America could no longer breathe.

They're still doing it. They've made it worse. To them, the 2016 election wasn't a signal that they're pissing a lot of people off with their nonsense about pronouns, "cultural appropriation" and "mansplaining." It was a call to arms, an alert that their work in getting everyone to conform isn't over and that it was time to redouble their efforts.

There isn't a more perfect example of that than what Elie Mystal, a Harvard-educated writer at the liberal *The Nation* magazine (the definition of being "oppressed"), said in 2020. Mystal wrote that he's "in a rage almost all the time," living in America. "If white people want to help, they can do what I do, and go fight the racists. Fight them in public, where everybody can see you. Fight them in private, where nobody can see you. Fight them at parties where I ain't invited. Fight them every day, at all times, everywhere."[5]

By "the racists," Mystal meant something more along the lines of everyday, well-intentioned Americans who don't live and dream thinking with race at the forefront of their minds. (In other words, anyone who doesn't identify as a liberal activist.)

It's very simple. Most Americans want to be able to talk, express themselves, even share innocent differences without the threat of being harassed, either in public or private, and especially at social events. At a minimum, we want to feel respected, not resented, for legitimately held beliefs. But therein lies the problem. Liberals don't

---

5 Mystal, Elie. "To the White People Who Keep Asking How to 'Help,'" *The Nation*, June 3, 2020. https://www.thenation.com/article/society/white-people-anti-racism/.

view all Americans as equals with honest disagreements. They view half, or even most of the country (depending on the topic) as offensive, unsophisticated, and illegitimate. To liberals, that part of the country doesn't deserve a moment's peace. They have work to do, fights to pick, and "privilege" to check.

"Fight them every day, at all times, everywhere."

You've almost certainly experienced the overwhelming, often intimidating torment of a liberal on the loose. You're not alone. That liberal Democrats naturally tend to be miserable is backed up by surveys, studies, and other data, all of which is covered extensively in the pages ahead.

Fortunately, we're not hopelessly consigned to simply bite our tongues and live with it. There are answers. But first, we have to understand the dark, dangerous, and unhappy setting of the liberal mind.

If you haven't done it already, brace yourself.

1

Democrats: Can't Live With 'Em, Can't Live Without 'Em Ruining Everything

Liberals and Democrats will never know the absolute crippling anxiety experienced by Right-wingers and otherwise normal people in social gatherings whenever politics or even mildly debatable topics come up. Although the average person would rather skip an argument and keep the party going with a more pleasant subjects, liberals and Democrats readily leap at the opportunity to tell you exactly how they feel, and, sorry, but *fuck you* if it's a problem.

What they have to say ruins the mood? Oh well! If you don't like it, you're wrong, and worse, a bad person who should feel very, very uncomfortable having shown up in the first place. And that's a best-case scenario. If you were to actually dispute what a liberal says, even in good nature, look forward to suffering while the Leftist gives you disgusted glances the rest of the evening and holds the incident against you for the rest of your life.

By contrast, Right-leaning Republicans tend to keep their mouths on mute when in mixed company. At most, one might politely disagree in such a situation. But if he does, he will say so in such a way that the liberal on the verge of making an embarrassing scene at least feels that their point of view has been acknowledged and that reasonable minds can disagree.

It's preciously naive because it's not enough. Leftists are miserable by nature, even if some of them are better at coping with it than their most insufferable peers.

This isn't a joke or an insult. It's proven. The way you have probably felt around these people, particularly within the last six years, is not in your head. It's a concrete reality borne out by endless data. You might even call it "The Science."

The easiest way to look at this is by simply asking two questions: are the happier, more tolerant, more forgiving people in America on the Left or on the Right? And why?

Like two plus two equaling four, or the ground getting wet when it rains, or all of Joy Reid's wigs looking ridiculously shiny on national television, the truth is self-evident. But it helps to back up assumptions with studies and statistics, so let's do that, starting with who is generally happier and more content.

Incidentally, scholars at the University of Florida and Toronto published an extensive study in 2011 titled in part, "Conservatives Are Happier Than Liberals, But Why?" That paper was based on yet several other studies surveying the attitudes of American adults on life and how those lined up with their political ideologies.[6]

In one survey, University of Florida students were asked questions about the control they felt over their own lives, their level of religiosity, moral principles, self-fulfillment, and also traditional political questions like the role of government versus the role of individuals in solving societal problems. The authors found that "conservatism

[6] Schlenker, B. R., et al. "Conservatives are happier than liberals, but why? Political ideology, personality, and life satisfaction." *Journal of Research in Personality*, 2012. https://labsites.rochester.edu/lelab/wp-content/uploads/2020/06/Schlenker-Chambers-Le-2012-Conservatives-are-happier-than-liberals-but-why-Political-ideology-personality-and-life-satisfaction.pdf.

was positively related to life satisfaction...and even after controlling for participants' age, gender, and family income level...conservatives are indeed happier than liberals." Surveyed students who were more likely to cite personal responsibility and conscientiousness as dominant factors in their lives tended to self-identify as politically conservative and also tended to exude "a more positive outlook and stronger feelings of self-worth, as indicated by greater optimism and self-esteem as well as lower depression and depressive symptomology."

Speaking of depression and other afflictions, the notion that Left-leaning people suffer more from mental illness is backed up by data as well, including a Pew Research Center survey in which liberals, regardless of race, were more likely to say that a doctor had diagnosed them with a mental health condition. They said so in greater numbers than both moderates and conservatives.

Zach Goldberg of the Center for the Study of Partisanship and Ideology looked at the results of a March 2020 Pew survey and found that among the self-identified "very liberal," 19 percent of nonwhite respondents said they had been told by a doctor at some point in their lives that they have "a mental health condition." Among "very liberal" whites, it's double that number.[7] Looking at self-identified "very conservative" respondents, though, the percentages are evenly split at just about 15 percent. The numbers aren't significantly different when you look at people identifying as just "conservative" versus "very conservative" and the same thing for just "liberal" versus "very liberal."[8]

Anyway, back to the "Conservatives are happier than liberals, but why?" study. Conservative students at the University of Florida tended to score higher on virtually every question related to self-satisfaction than their counterparts on the Left. The authors

---

7 Goldberg, Zach. Twitter, April 11, 2020. https://threadreaderapp.com/thread/1248823584111439872.html.

8 "Most Americans Say Coronavirus Outbreak Has Impacted Their Lives," Pew Research Center, March 30, 2020. https://www.pewresearch.org/social-trends/2020/03/30/most-americans-say-coronavirus-outbreak-has-impacted-their-lives/.

said that conservatives scored higher on questions related to "duty" and "honor," as well as "personal commitment," and on matters of "national strength," like the rule of law and national security. The study made no judgment as to whether there was anything wrong, per se, with liberals, but only observed that conservatives tended to exhibit qualities consistent with a more fulfilled life than did liberals.

As the authors put it, the study "showed that personality and attitude measures traditionally associated with positive adjustment—personal agency, positive outlook, and transcendent moral beliefs—can account for why conservatives are happier than liberals."

A second study in that paper used the 2010 World Values Survey, which is conducted by scientists around the globe every five years. The authors used publicly available data from the survey related to US adults and their various dispositions, like political ideology, life satisfaction, personal control and religiosity. The authors found that "conservatism was…related to life satisfaction overall," which included a correlation between Right-leaning people and a heightened sense of self-esteem, optimism, and "better mental health."They observed that, "Conservatives are not only happier with life in general, but also they are happier with their marriages, family relationships, jobs, financial situations, health, and even where they reside." This remained true even when factors related to income, education, age, and gender were eliminated.

In other words, participants identifying as conservative, regardless of how much money they made, their age, where they went to school, and whether they were male or female, professed to having a greater sense of well-being than participants who identified as liberal.

Lest there be any doubt about any of this, Gallup found in 2007 that "Republicans are significantly more likely than Democrats or independents to rate their mental health as excellent." A wide majority, 58 percent, of Republicans rated their own mental health as "excellent." By contrast, only 38 percent of Democrats said the same.[9]

That's more or less the same that Gallup found in a survey three years earlier. "Republicans are more likely to report having excellent mental health than are independents and, in particular, Democrats," the report said. In that survey, 62 percent of Republicans attested to having "excellent" mental health versus 40 percent of Democrats.[10]

On the question of marriage, the General Social Survey, conducted by the University of Chicago from 2010 to 2014, had conservatives reporting a higher percentage than liberals in saying that they were happily married. It was a twelve-point difference.[11]

Back once again to the "Conservatives are happier than liberals, but why?" study. A third analysis included in that paper looked at data provided by the aforementioned General Social Survey of 2010 and found that "conservatives have personality and attitude characteristics that are usually associated with positive adjustment and mental health." They determined this using individual self-assessment of areas that would generally be related to happiness, like a person's marriage, family, where he lives, his job, hobbies, and personal health. Those who fell into the conservative column were significantly more likely to be satisfied in every category, other than in "hobbies and leisure activities" (which I assume liberals cling to with a vice grip in order to distract themselves from their otherwise empty lives—and do they really love trail hiking that much?).

A lazy critic might dismiss the findings as the result of a couple Right-wing academics (because those are everywhere!) who had an

---

9 Newport, Frank. "Republicans Report Much Better Mental Health Than Others," *Gallup*, Nov. 30, 2007. https://news.gallup.com/poll/102943/republicans-report-much-better-mental-health-than-others.aspx.

10 Newport, Frank. "Assessing Americans' Mental Health," *Gallup*, Dec. 2, 2004. https://news.gallup.com/poll/14218/assessing-americans-mental-health.aspx.

11 Wilcox, W. Bradford. "More than Money: The Liberal-Conservative Divide in Marriage," Institute for Family Studies, Sep. 1, 2015. https://ifstudies.org/blog/more-than-money-the-liberal-conservative-divide-in-marriage/.

agenda and used dubious methods to crunch numbers for a preferred outcome. Okay, but to believe that would mean ignoring the mountains of data elsewhere that all point to the same thing—that liberals are just not happy people and, in fact, display tendencies to indicate maladjustment.

Rather than communicate like normal adults who can hear each other out and, at minimum, reach an understanding of differences, the immediate impulse of liberals is fight or flight. For liberals, political disagreements aren't opportunities to learn or engage. To the contrary, they see those disputes as reasons to shrink their social circles, withdraw from family, and silo themselves with others who will say only things that affirm their bitchy predispositions and won't disrupt their weird mentality.

A December 2016 survey by the Public Religion Research Institute showed a quarter of Democrats attesting to having blocked, unfriended, or stopped "following" someone on social media after the year's election because of something political that the person posted. Only 9 percent of Republicans said the same. The Institute further noted that self-identified, ideological liberals were "far more likely"—by twenty points—to say they removed someone from their social media circle based on something they said.[12]

A reasonable guess might be that Republicans were less temperamental because their team had just won the presidency. Everyone can surely recall just how sour Democrats were in the days, months, and years that followed, having unexpectedly seen Empress Hillary vanquished by the unlikeliest of heroes. When your football team wins, you're in a better mood.

But the results in the Institute's survey have been replicated elsewhere, even during what you might assume would be happier times for liberals and Democrats.

---

12 Cox, Daniel and Jones, Robert P. PhD. "'Merry Christmas' vs. 'Happy Holidays': Republicans and Democrats are Polar Opposites," Public Religion Research Institute, Dec. 19, 2016. https://www.prri.org/research/poll-post-election-holiday-war-christmas/.

A survey by Pew from 2014, when Democrats were in control of the White House, echoed the Institute, though Pew's analysis was with regard to activity only on Facebook. Among users who hid, blocked, or unfriended a person because of something political they posted and disagreed with, 44 percent of them identified as "consistent liberals." By contrast, 31 percent identified as "consistent conservatives," a thirteen-point difference.[13]

Another Pew survey from 2012, at which point Democrats were still in control of the White House, asked more broadly about social networking websites. And again, it found that liberals were most likely to have blocked, unfriended, or hidden someone over their political posts. For conservatives, 16 percent said they had taken all of those measures. For liberals, though, it was 28 percent, a twelve-point difference.[14]

The intolerance, bitterness, and spite of liberals manifest just as well offline. They're also more likely to say they've socially iced out real-life friends over political disagreements, that they would rather not associate with people who don't think like them, and that romantic relationships with political opposites are a nonstarter.

The American Perspectives Survey, conducted in May 2021 by the Survey Center on American Life, found Democrats and liberals were more likely to say they have ended friendships because of political disagreement. Among Republicans, 10 percent said they had done so. It was double for Democrats. In terms of ideology, 28 percent of liberals said they had ended friendships over political disagreements. Only 10 percent of conservatives said the same.[15]

---

[13] "Political Polarization & Media Habits," Pew Research Center, Oct. 21, 2014. https://www.pewresearch.org/journalism/2014/10/21/political-polarization-media-habits/.

[14] "Social networking sites and politics," Pew Research Center, March 12, 2012. https://www.pewresearch.org/internet/2012/03/12/main-findings-10/.

[15] Cox, Daniel A. "The State of American Friendship: Change, Challenges, and Loss," Survey Center on American Life, June 8, 2021. https://www.americansurveycenter.org/research/the-state-of-american-friendship-change-challenges-and-loss/.

Relatedly, Pew Research in February 2020 reported that liberals were more likely than conservatives, 60 percent to 45 percent, respectively, to say that they had stopped talking about news centered on politics and the upcoming election with an individual because of something that the person said.[16]

As much as you have something to say, liberals just as assuredly don't want to hear it. This wouldn't be so annoying if they didn't pretend to place so much value on tolerance and diversity. Liberals are nothing if not close-minded, insolent grumps.

In July 2017, a separate Pew survey showed that 35 percent of Democrats said the previous year's election put a strain on their relationships with friends who they knew voted for Trump. Only 13 percent of Republicans said the same about friends who voted for Clinton.[17]

In October of that year, the libertarian CATO Institute asked US adults whether they believed it was hard to be friends with someone who supported either Trump or Clinton. Among those who voted for Clinton, more than 60 percent said it would be hard to be friends with someone who supported her opponent. For Trump voters, the number was nearly cut in half to 34 percent who said it would be hard to be friends with a Clinton supporter.[18]

At some point, this isn't just a matter of sour grapes. It's pathological.

---

16 Jurkowitz, Mark and Mitchell, Amy. "A sore subject: Almost half of Americans have stopped talking politics with someone," Pew Research Center, Feb. 5, 2020. https://www.pewresearch.org/journalism/2020/02/05/a-sore-subject-almost-half-of-americans-have-stopped-talking-politics-with-someone/.

17 "Since Trump's Election, Increased Attention to Politics—Especially Among Women," Pew Research Center, July 20, 2017. https://www.pewresearch.org/politics/2017/07/20/since-trumps-election-increased-attention-to-politics-especially-among-women/1_51-2/.

18 Ekins, Emily. "The State of Free Speech and Tolerance in America," Cato Institute, Oct. 31, 2017. https://www.cato.org/blog/poll-71-americans-say-political-correctness-has-silenced-discussions-society-needs-have-58.

An NBC poll from September 2018, just over 35 percent of Democrats said they would be uncomfortable, at least to some degree, having close Republican friends. Only 21 percent of Republicans said the same of Democrats. By contrast, 44 percent of Republicans said they would be "very comfortable" with a close friend who was a Democrat. Only 26 percent of Democrats would say the same for Republicans.[19]

The University of North Carolina published a survey in March 2020 that asked students whether they would mind having a friend who was politically opposite. An overwhelming majority of Republicans, 92 percent, said they were unopposed. Far fewer Democrats, 63 percent, agreed.[20]

Republicans: The more the merrier!

Democrats: Actually, can you show me proof of vaccination?

Surveys at Dartmouth University have had similar results. In 2018, the campus newspaper asked students a series of questions about socializing with people who were political opposites of them.[21] Across the board, self-identified Democrats were more likely to say they would not consider befriending (55 percent versus 12 percent of Republicans), trusting (39 percent versus 10 percent of Republicans) studying with (23 percent versus 7 percent of Republicans), or working on a class project with (22 percent versus 8 percent of Republicans) a person who is the political opposite.

A survey the previous year at the school asked students how comfortable they would be having a roommate who was politically

---

19 Seitz-Wald, Alex. "Mad About Trump," *NBC News*, Sep. 4, 2018. https://www.nbcnews.com/specials/mad-about-trump/.

20 Larson, et al., Jennifer. "Free Expression and Constructive Dialogue at the University of North Carolina at Chapel Hill," UNC Chapel Hill, March 2, 2020. https://fecdsurveyreport.web.unc.edu/wp-content/uploads/sites/22160/2020/02/UNC-Free-Expression-Report.pdf.

21 Zhou, Amanda and Agadjanian, Alexander. "A survey of Dartmouth's political and free speech climate," the *Dartmouth*, May 22, 2018. https://www.thedartmouth.com/article/2018/05/a-survey-of-dartmouths-political-and-free-speech-climate.

opposite. Again, liberals were more likely to say that such a setup would make them uncomfortable, 45 percent versus just 12 percent of Republicans.[22]

Liberals don't want to be your roommate if you don't think like them. They don't want to study with you. They don't want you as a close friend. They don't want to hear what you have to say. They'd rather not look at you, if they can help it.

Good luck if you're a Right-winger who might want to ask out an attractive liberal. (It's rumored that they exist.) They don't want to do that, either. The aforementioned survey at the University of North Carolina had also asked about dating. A majority of conservative students, 56 percent, said they wouldn't mind dating someone who was their political opposite. For liberals, it was only 25 percent. Furthermore, the 2018 Dartmouth survey had 82 percent of Democrats saying they would not consider dating a Republican, versus 42 percent of Republicans who said the same of Democrats.

In that not-so-common event that you did make it along with a liberal romantically, don't assume you'll have a fun time with the in-laws. If their parents were also liberal, be prepared for them to hate you, a possibility that's more likely than if they were conservatives.

A 2019 survey by Public Religion Research Institute had 45 percent of Democrats saying that they would be at least somewhat unhappy if their child married a Republican. Among Republicans, a smaller percentage, 35 percent, said the same about Democrats.[23]

A YouGov survey conducted three years prior similarly asked Democrats and Republicans if they would be upset about their child marrying someone politically opposite. Nearly a quarter of Democrats

---

22 Zhou, Amanda and Agadjanian, Alexander. "A survey of Dartmouth's political landscape," the *Dartmouth*, April 16, 2017. https://www.thedartmouth.com/article/2017/04/a-survey-of-dartmouths-political-landscape.

23 Najle, Ph.D, Maxine and Jones, Ph.D., Robert P. "American Democracy in Crisis: The Fate of Pluralism in a Divided Nation," Public Religion Research Institute, Feb. 19, 2019. https://www.prri.org/research/american-democracy-in-crisis-the-fate-of-pluralism-in-a-divided-nation/.

said that they would be upset if their child married a conservative. Just 16 percent of Republicans said the same if their child married a liberal.[24]

The numbers make clear that not all liberals are necessarily assholes. But if someone is a liberal, they're much more likely to be an asshole. It's their essence. It's in their DNA. Bitter is their natural state of being. Unpleasant is their default position.

They have little to no interest in associating with people who don't see the world as they do.

Save it. They don't want to hear it. The block button is their favorite feature.

It's not even clear that they can help themselves. Every indication is that it's a form of psychoneurosis. Why else would anyone choose to limit their own options for friends, lovers, and other beneficial connections over something that is intended to be resolved not by personal conflict but by elections?

Don't like the way the last one turned out? Good thing for you, liberals, that there's one every two years. Quit worrying. It's okay to smile in between.

The most advantageous part of our democracy is intentionally neglected by liberals and Democrats. It figures. But they have a hard time seeing the good in anything.

---

[24] Dahlgreen, Will. "Left-wingers like to keep it in the family," *YouGov*, Feb. 10, 2016. https://web.archive.org/web/20181021040602/https://yougov.co.uk/news/2016/02/10/left-wingers-keep-family/.

2

The Left Loved the Pandemic and They Wanted You to Love It, Too

Nothing quite revealed what absolutely horrific human beings that liberals could be quite like the COVID pandemic. The annoying things they've always done—nag, whine, lecture, tattle—came with the most precious gift in 2020: the backing, approval and moral authority of the state, as it's conceived in the Left's mind.

With the sanction of the government to insert themselves in everyone else's business, liberals felt free to pole vault atop the highest soap box and reign down their most wretched sanctimony—all in the name of "The Science."

From their greatest hits list:

- "Where's your mask?"
- "You're putting others at risk."
- "Why are you traveling?"
- "Stay home!"
- "We're all in this together."

- "Follow the science!"
- "Trust the science!"
- "Six feet apart!"
- "Practice social distancing!"
- "Why don't you wear your mask." (Always phrased as a question, even though it wasn't.)

Insufferable is the word.

It was like the end of *Grease* when Sandy—formerly a plain Jane, now donning a leather jacket and makeup—suddenly has the balls to act like she runs the place. Except the audience loves Sandy for going the extra mile to win a love interest. Liberals were simply acting out their wildest wet dreams of being able to tell everyone what to do, snapping at innocent people while feeling good about themselves. Nobody loved that or the people acting it out.

This remained true even into 2021. In March of that year, a full year after the initial pandemic alarm hit the US, Democrats, liberals were still hyperventilating over its spread: 82 percent of Democrats and Democrat-leaning voters believed the new coronavirus was a "major threat" to the entire US population "as a whole," according to a Pew Research survey. Just half as many Republicans, 41 percent, agreed. This was well after learning that COVID was relatively harmless to the vast majority of us, with something like a 98 percent survival rate.[25]

The same survey had an obscene number of Democrats, 93 percent, who said people should still avoid gathering in large groups. Among Republicans it was 56 percent, a large portion of which had been no doubt conditioned to say the Right Things™ in public when it comes to COVID. By this time, there were three highly effective

---

[25] Funk, Cary and Tyson, Alec. "Growing Share of Americans Say They Plan To Get a COVID-19 Vaccine—or Already Have," Pew Research Center, March 5, 2021. https://www.pewresearch.org/science/2021/03/05/growing-share-of-americans-say-they-plan-to-get-a-covid-19-vaccine-or-already-have/.

vaccines available and yet liberals were still pestering people about wearing masks, not gathering in crowds, and avoiding anything formerly known as "fun."

Heading into the spring of 2021, with vaccines at the ready, even Democrat-run states were reopening at a rapid pace. And yet, like former high school jocks who know they're past their peak, the liberals were desperate for yesterday.

Pew asked US adults the same question nearly a year apart (May of 2020 and then again in February of 2021) whether they thought there should be fewer, more, or about the same amount of restrictions in their location due to an outbreak of COVID. Among Democrats, those who wanted more restrictions between May 2020 and February 2021 went up, from 35 percent to 41 percent. For Republicans, it went down, from 16 percent to 12 percent.

That's right: a year after the initial spread of the coronavirus, at which point hospitals were far better equipped at treating the infected, and with the widespread (*free!*) availability of (*three!*) highly effective vaccines, Democrats wanted more lockdowns.

They couldn't let it go because to recognize the truth that there was no stopping an insanely contagious, airborne virus, one that passed through almost everyone without incident, would be to give up their purpose in life, which is to control people and force us into the same state of misery as them.

As of this writing, there were about 70,600,000 confirmed cases of COVID in the US, according to the *New York Times.* And there had been about 866,000 deaths. That puts the survivability of an infection at 98.8 percent.

Whatever you think of vaccines—I don't care who gets one or who doesn't—the numbers show them to be successful at reducing your risk of severe illness from COVID. But it was still supposed to be national news in early October 2021 that Supreme Court Justice Brett Kavanaugh and other vaccinated people tested positive for

COVID. Kavanaugh wasn't even showing symptoms but CNN,[26] NPR,[27] the *New York Times*,[28] and the Associated Press[29] each dedicated stories to his infection.

Kavanaugh, like almost everyone else, recovered just fine. Nobody should be asked to care about any of it.

If Anthony Fauci got COVID because he was maskless at a strip club, that would have been an interesting pandemic story. Aside from that, the someone-got-COVID story was played out.

But Democrats and the media have spent more than two years keeping the country on the brink about the virus, doing their best to ensure that everyone remains in a perpetual state of anxiety and fear.

It's true that we're rapidly closing in on one million deaths from the virus. That isn't nothing. It's a tragedy. Most who perished were elderly. Those were lives cut too short nonetheless. Anyone can see that. But liberals saw beyond the tragedy. They saw opportunity.

Even after the pandemic was effectively over—which was as soon as vaccines were available in December 2020—liberals insisted that we act as if it wasn't. Don't travel! Six feet apart! Stay Home™!

Getting through the pandemic would mean getting back to normal, which is something Democrats and the media only sometimes pretended to wish for. Most of the time, though, they were practically cheering on the new coronavirus.

---

26 de Vries, Karl and Stracqualursi, Veronica. "Justice Brett Kavanaugh tests positive for Covid-19," CNN.com, Oct. 1, 2021. https://www.cnn.com/2021/10/01/politics/brett-kavanaugh-covid-19/index.html.

27 Calamur, Krishnadev. "Justice Kavanaugh tests positive for COVID, Supreme Court says," NPR.org, Oct. 1, 2021. https://www.npr.org/2021/10/01/1042269542/justice-kavanaugh-tests-positive-for-covid-supreme-court-says.

28 Liptak, Adam. "Justice Kavanaugh tests positive for the virus," *New York Times*, Oct. 1, 2021. https://www.nytimes.com/2021/10/01/us/politics/brett-kavanaugh-covid.html.

29 Gresko, Jessica, and Sherman, Mark. "Justice Kavanaugh tests positive for COVID, has no symptoms," *Associated Press*, Oct. 1, 2021. https://apnews.com/article/coronavirus-pandemic-health-amy-coney-barrett-courts-us-supreme-court-5c24ffb572dd34a8b24f226fc2211b7a.

They believed that more spread meant additional mandates, and there's nothing liberals love more than a good government mandate (other than calling unassuming people "racist," their first love).

And that's why the *New York Times* opinion page had become the place for a steady stream of peppy pieces on how great masks, restrictions, and higher prices really were, in light of the pandemic.

To wit, the paper ran a column in August 2021 looking at all the upsides of making children smother half their faces while in school. "Wearing a mask can also help teach children to pay more attention to their own bodies and physical behaviors," wrote Judith Danovitch, a professor at the University of Louisville. "Keeping a mask on over the course of a school day involves the kind of self-control and self-regulation that many children find challenging. Younger children must inhibit the urge to pull off their mask, and older children must be mindful of when their mask is slipping down or when it's OK to take it off."[30]

See that, moms and dads? It's not just a mask. It's an educational tool!

Shortly before that little number, the *Times* ran a separate piece authored by a restaurant owner actually encouraging people to eat out less and at the same time, welcome higher menu prices. "Adjusting to the price of better work cultures will be difficult for many," wrote Peter Hoffman. "But dining out less isn't necessarily a bad thing. Treating a restaurant meal as a special occasion rather than a frequent convenience may represent a quality of life improvement for all."[31]

The pandemic has become a religion for these people. Hoffman owns his own fine eateries where he could very easily raise menu prices

---

30 Danovitch, Judith. "Actually, Wearing a Mask Can Help Your Child Learn," *New York Times*, Aug. 18, 2021. https://www.nytimes.com/2021/08/18/opinion/masks-schools-covid.html.

31 Hoffman, Peter. "Restaurants Will Never Be the Same. They Shouldn't Be," *New York Times*, Aug. 10, 2021. https://www.nytimes.com/2021/08/10/opinion/restaurants-covid-pandemic.html.

and begin a "quality of life improvement for all" of his own staff. But that's not enough. He wants to make converts out of everyone else.

Hoffman's reasoning was that restaurants are often less-than-ideal places to work. That's probably true. So are landfills. But what does it have to do with me or anyone else who enjoys frequently dining out? He was free to lead by example and pay his servers more, plus treat them better as he saw fit.

But it's a pandemic! Didn't you like it when restaurants tacked on special COVID fees, forced you to eat outside, or only served pickup orders? That was a quality-of-life improvement for all!

It's been obvious for a long time that Democrats and the media had been enjoying the coronavirus. It ensured that people stayed home and relied on a government checks. That's the stuff their dreams are made of. Lockdowns mean more welfare and, more importantly, less energy consumption. They believe that's better for the planet, which to them is far more urgent than your personal ambitions or your hopes to see friends, family, and places that aren't within walking distance.

Professional nag Farhad Manjoo of the *Times* wrote in July 2021 that even as it became safer to resume normal air travel, thanks to vaccine distribution, maybe, really, truly, honestly, you'd better not. "Sure, there's something magical about meeting face to face, but in an age of pretty good videoconferencing, there isn't magic enough to justify the extreme environmental costs of routine flight," he said. "But flying is so carbon intensive—your share of the emissions from a single round-trip trans-Atlantic flight are almost enough to wipe out the gains you might get from living car-free for a year—that it's worth considering limiting leisure plane trips, too."[32]

The phrase "it's worth considering" is liberal speak for, "Do as I say, moron."

32 Manjoo, Farhad. "Summer Travel Is Back. Earth Can't Handle It," *New York Times*, July 8, 2021. https://www.nytimes.com/2021/07/08/opinion/travel-covid-climate-change.html.

New York Times TV critic James Poniewozik thought it was a real shame that after two years, fictional television shows seemed to think it was probably a good time to move on. "[M]aybe most awkward," he wrote in early January 2022, "have been the series that acknowledged Covid existed but declared or implied it was over long before Covid decided it was over."[33]

Poniewozik appeared on MSNBC's *Morning Joe* to elaborate. He said he had noticed an "unsettling phenomenon where shows are sort of taking the standpoint where, okay, in the world of our show, the pandemic did happen and it existed and it was a real thing but now it's over."[34] The lack of pandemic references, Poniewozik said, presented the message that, "It somehow got fixed, yada, yada, yada, and the rest of you are on your own." He said the dearth of virus acknowledgement "often ends up being kind of a more unsettling thing than never acknowledging the pandemic in the first place."

The poor guy. His brain was so consumed by the virus that spending a few moments escaped in a TV show was now more disturbing to him than covering up his nose and mouth when out in public.

Democrats occasionally would say something about going back to "normal," but that's not really what they wanted. They had been loving COVID too much.

If Democrats were really so concerned with eradicating the virus, they might have said a word or two about the leader of their party's abysmal performance on the issue. It was Joe Biden who declared with unwavering confidence that he would "shut down the virus" if only voters would put him in the White House.

Well, they did that, and Biden had the great fortune of being sworn into office with three vaccines ready for distribution and a national infection rate that was plummeting.

---

33 Poniewozik, Jamie. "Wondering When the Pandemic Will End? On TV, It Already Has," *New York Times*, Jan. 7, 2021. https://www.nytimes.com/2022/01/07/arts/television/tv-shows-covid-pandemic.html.

34 Poniewozik, Jamie. "How Some TV Shows Are Putting The Pandemic In The Past," MSNBC's "Morning Joe," Jan. 10, 2022.

It took him less than six months to squander it. Thanks to Democrats, including Biden and his vice president, having spent 2020 casting doubt on any vaccine developed under the previous administration—after all, they had an election to win, even if it meant people would die—a sizable chunk of the population vulnerable to the virus was resistant to getting shots. There were plenty of legitimate reasons to decline receiving a vaccine, like having built up antibodies through natural infection or having concerns about infertility, but many people were abstaining out of both spite for political reasons, and fear because Democratic leaders had explicitly said they couldn't trust a medicine greenlit by Trump.

Here's what Vice President Kamala Harris said on September 6, 2020: "I will say that I would not trust Donald Trump. And it would have to be a credible source of information that talks about the efficacy and the reliability of whatever he's talking about. I will not take his word for it. He wants us to inject bleach. I—no, I will not take his word."[35]

President Joe Biden said on August 6, 2020: "The way [Trump] talks about the vaccine is not particularly rational. He's talking about it being ready, he's going to talk about moving it quicker than the scientists think it should be moved…People don't believe that he's telling the truth, therefore they're not at all certain they're going to take the vaccine. And one more thing: if and when the vaccine comes, it's not likely to go through all the tests that need to be done, and the trials that are needed to be done."[36]

Despite those remarks, the "fact-checking" website PolitiFact laughably said it was "false" to claim that Biden and Harris were sowing doubt on vaccines. "Their full statements show," the site said, "they were raising doubts about Trump's trustworthiness, his ability

---

[35] Harris, Kamala. CNN's "State of the Union," Sep. 6, 2020. http://transcripts.cnn.com/TRANSCRIPTS/2009/06/sotu.01.html.

[36] Biden, Joe. Press conference, Aug. 6, 2020. https://www.youtube.com/watch?v=iCpyx2T-lDA&t=863s.

to roll out the vaccines safely and the risk of political influence over vaccine development."[37]

If a political leader is warning, without evidence, that a medicine might be unsafe based on who's in the White House, why wouldn't many people opt not to inject themselves with it once it's available? If Democrats were telling voters to be suspicious of any vaccine produced under the Trump administration, why should Republicans have not been equally skeptical under a new Democrat one?

And after all that, the first thing Democrats did after Biden's inauguration was complain that all the work he said he would do on the pandemic wasn't already completed.

Longtime Washington journalist Mike Allen hurled a fast one at Harris when he asked her a month after she was sworn in what she had found "harder" than expected in addressing the pandemic. "Like, how are you finding the hole is deeper?" said Allen.

"There was no stockpile…of vaccines, right?" Harris replied. "So, we're looking at this. There was no national strategy or plan for vaccinations. We were leaving it to states and local leaders to try and figure it out, and so in many ways, we are starting from scratch on something that's been raging for almost an entire year."[38]

Why, exactly, would Harris have been under the impression that there would be a "stockpile" of vaccine for her and President Biden to start passing out once sworn into office? The point of rushing production and government approval of any vaccine was for direct distribution to the public that needed it, which is what happened once the medicines were approved for emergency use in December 2020. It was never part of the mission to hoard mass doses of the drug for Harris and Biden to find after entering the White House.

---

[37] Kertscher, Tom. "Biden, Harris distrusted Trump with COVID-19 vaccines, not the vaccines themselves," PolitiFact, July 23, 2021. https://www.politifact.com/factchecks/2021/jul/23/tiktok-posts/biden-harris-doubted-trump-covid-19-vaccines-not-v/.

[38] Harris, Kamala. HBO's "Axios," Feb. 14, 2021. https://www.youtube.com/watch?v=3Om3or2YwTw.

Imagine what the media would have said if Trump had been stockpiling vaccines while thousands of people continued to die each day.

Harris might be lazy and incompetent, but she isn't entirely retarded. She knows there is absolutely no reason for there to have been stored vaccines that had been on the United States market for only two months and that every country in the world was trying to distribute to its population as quickly as possible.

To Harris's second point about there being "no national strategy or plan for vaccinations" because "we were leaving it to states and local leaders to try and figure it out," it's as if Democrats are completely ignorant about the purposes of mayors and governors. They exist for precisely these moments, and their job isn't to serve as dead weight. They're supposed to govern their states and cities and, if necessary, ask for additional support at the federal level.

This is actually a fairly large country, and people huddled in Washington, D.C., aren't equipped to parachute into every city and county to fix all of their problems. Again, that's the purpose of mayors and governors.

Lastly, the new administration wasn't "starting from scratch." The sainted Dr. Anthony Fauci denied it the first time CNN dutifully reported that false claim by an anonymous White House official[39] (for the obvious purpose of lowering public expectations for the administration).[40]

White House Senior Advisor Cedric Richmond in January 2021 had also tried making the stupid claim that, "The last administration didn't leave anything. They didn't leave a plan."[41]

---

[39] Weixel, Nathaniel. "Fauci: We are not 'starting from scratch' on vaccine distribution," The Hill, Jan. 21, 2021. https://thehill.com/policy/healthcare/535327-fauci-we-are-not-starting-from-scratch-on-vaccine-distribution.

[40] Lee, MJ. "Biden inheriting nonexistent coronavirus vaccine distribution plan and must start 'from scratch,' sources say," CNN.com, Jan. 21, 2021. https://www.cnn.com/2021/01/21/politics/biden-covid-vaccination-trump/index.html.

[41] Richmond, Cedric. CNN's "Newsroom," Jan. 23, 2021. https://twitter.com/mj_lee/status/1353350434963017729.

But even if the administration was being thrown into the deep end, Biden claimed all along that he was the lifeboat.

"We're eight months into this pandemic, and Donald Trump still doesn't have a plan to get this virus under control. I do."—Joe Biden, October 15, 2020.[42]

All Biden and Harris had been doing since even before the inauguration was complain that the problem hadn't already been solved for them. Democrats are allowed to do that, though. The media let them.

Biden and Harris weren't capable of doing anything that would even stall the virus's spread, let alone cut it off completely. They could only push their precious vaccines, their beloved masks, and their horny fetish for restricting social activities.

Immediately upon taking office, Biden launched a ridiculous "100 Days Masking Challenge" wherein he asked Americans to perform their "patriotic duty" and "mask up for 100 days."[43]

More than a year later, on January 24, 2022, Biden pleaded to the public to "wear a mask" because, he said, "It's an important tool to help stop the spread" of the more contagious Omicron virus variant.[44] That marked day 369 of the 100 Days Masking Challenge. Where's our prize?

Biden and the Democrat-run Congress were quick to pass a bloated spending bill with a price tag of $2 trillion that they had said was desperately needed to keep the economy afloat and fight the unabated spread. But it wasn't so much intended to beat back the virus as it was to keep people out of work by giving them obscene amounts

---

[42] Biden, Joe. Twitter, Oct. 15, 2020. https://twitter.com/joebiden/status/1316894374500962305?lang=en.

[43] "Fact Sheet: President-elect Biden's Day One Executive Actions Deliver Relief for Families Across America Amid Converging Crises," White House, Jan. 20, 2021. https://www.whitehouse.gov/briefing-room/statements-releases/2021/01/20/fact-sheet-president-elect-bidens-day-one-executive-actions-deliver-relief-for-families-across-america-amid-converging-crises/.

[44] Biden, Joe. Twitter, Jan. 24, 2022. https://twitter.com/JoeBiden/status/1485645579682304002.

of cash to stay home, the result of which was a frustrating, persistent labor shortage and skyrocketing gas and food prices to boot.

And so, after months of a declining rate of infections, and even with a majority of the country having been vaccinated, beginning in early July, Biden oversaw only then the second-worst wave of new infection rates since the start of the pandemic. On July 5, we were averaging 10,608 new cases each day. By the middle of September, that number had multiplied by almost seventeen, soaring to 175,822.

In that same period, we were averaging a couple hundred COVID-related deaths each day. By mid-September, the number was 1,618. In no time, we reached more than two thousand deaths per day.[45]

All the while, Biden looked like Mr. Magoo, first coming into office and begging people to wear masks for one hundred days, then telling them to keep them on indefinitely. That gimmick apparently didn't quite do the trick. Who knew?!

The vaccines were the promised ticket back to normalcy. But then Biden told even the vaccinated to wear masks. If they flew out of the country and were infected abroad, they were not allowed to fly back until they rendered a negative test. That's apparently what it means to "shut down the virus."

All the data show that vaccines are highly effective in keeping people out of the hospital, but Biden was telling everyone who had done what they were told would keep them safe that their lives could be no different than anyone else.

Recall the president's panicked, premature vow in the fall of 2021 to make "booster shots" available to everyone "across the board," only to have his own Food and Drug Administration turn him down,

---

45 "Trends in Number of COVID-19 Cases and Deaths in the US Reported to CDC, by State/Territory," Centers for Disease Control and Prevention. https://covid.cdc.gov/covid-data-tracker/#trends_dailydeaths.

determining that not everyone should get yet more pharmaceuticals pumped into their bodies.[46]

The incompetence was awe-inspiring.

At a White House briefing in September, a reporter asked Biden how much of the population would need to be vaccinated in order to "go back to normal."[47] The president said as much as 98 percent. He might as well have said, "Wishful thinking."

At the time, only 55 percent of the population had been fully vaccinated and the *New York Times* estimated that at the pace we were going, it wouldn't be until late July of 2022 that just 85 percent of the eligible public ages twelve and up might have received one dose of vaccine.[48]

Americans understandably grew tired of it. Liberals had obnoxiously claimed all along that they were the ones who "follow the science" and "listen to the experts." They won the 2020 election and under their leadership, they made it all dramatically worse.

In March 2021, Biden had said that "if we do our part" there was "a good chance" that families and friends could have "small groups" for an Independence Day outdoor barbecue. Fast-forward to October and Dr. Anthony Fauci, Biden's top COVID adviser and the media's favorite sex symbol, was telling people he wasn't sure they could

---

46 Shear, Michael and Mueller, Benjamin. "Biden Promised to Follow the Science. But Sometimes, He Gets Ahead of the Experts," *New York Times*, Sep. 24, 2021. https://www.nytimes.com/2021/09/24/us/politics/biden-science-boosters-vaccine.html.

47 Fleetwood, Shawn. "Biden All But Admits He's Never Letting the U.S. Return to a Pre-COVID Normal," the *Federalist*, Sep. 27, 2021. https://thefdrlst.wpengine.com/2021/09/27/biden-all-but-admits-hes-never-letting-the-u-s-return-to-a-pre-covid-normal/.

48 "See How Vaccinations Are Going in Your County and State," *New York Times*. https://www.nytimes.com/interactive/2020/us/covid-19-vaccine-doses.html.

gather for Christmas (only to reverse shortly thereafter to say never mind, they could!).[49]

Almost no one could answer whether a vaccine booster shot was a good idea for themselves. In mid-August, Biden said at the White House that there was "a plan for booster shots to every fully vaccinated American—adult American" and that those shots would be available the week of September 20. Then the FDA said nope!

A couple of days before Biden's September 20 deadline, the FDA declined to approve boosters for most adults, instead stating that only adults over sixty-five, plus anyone deemed "high risk," should get an additional shot.[50]

Unfortunately, that wasn't any less confusing. Is any given individual high risk or not? It turns out to not really matter. If you wanted a shot, you could get one. Plenty of people did it, regardless of risk status. Did they need it? Who knows! Best of luck!

What about the godforsaken masks? Biden didn't wait a moment after being sworn in to tell the public that he was asking them to "mask up" for "100 days." And yet coming up on three hundred days later, the public was still being told by his Centers for Disease Control and Prevention that regardless of whether a person had received a vaccine, he should be wearing a mask when in public.

In that time, Biden's administration went from telling the vaccinated to continue wearing masks to then saying that wasn't necessary, to going back to advising face coverings again.

It was precisely the kind of instability we were told not to expect from Biden. He was supposedly the remedy to his predecessor's "chaos."

---

49 Chamberlain, Samuel. "Fauci now says Americans can meet family for Christmas—as he will," *New York Post*, Oct. 4, 2021. https://nypost.com/2021/10/04/fauci-now-says-americans-can-meet-family-for-christmas/.

50 Miller, Sara G., Lewis, Reynolds, and Edwards, Erika. "FDA advisory group rejects Covid boosters for most, limits to high-risk groups," NBCNews.com, Sep. 17, 2021. https://www.nbcnews.com/health/health-news/fda-advisory-group-rejects-covid-boosters-limits-high-risk-groups-rcna2074.

Biden's handling of the pandemic had by every measure been a complete catastrophe. People noticed, no doubt sensing that their lives weren't getting any better as they headed three years into this nonsense. An Axios-Ipsos poll released in late September 2021 showed that less than half of US adults, 45 percent, said they believed they could trust Biden "a great deal" or "fair amount" to provide them with accurate information on the pandemic. That was a thirteen-point drop from January, when 58 percent of those surveyed said they felt they could trust him.[51]

If it seemed of little concern to Democrats, that's because it was. While simultaneously hectoring everyone about "putting others at risk" for going to visit their grandparents for the holidays, they behaved in their own private lives as if there was no pandemic at all. It was the opposite. They were having a great time.

Biden himself was seen in late October 2021 traipsing through Georgetown Italian restaurant Fiola Mare (where you can get an eighty-dollar plate of pasta) without a mask.[52] It was in direct violation of an ordinance in Washington, D.C., expressly requiring restaurant patrons to wear a face covering unless seated and actively eating or drinking. Not to mention that it also went against the guidance of his own CDC that also recommended indoor mask wearing. White House Press Secretary Jen Psaki brushed criticism away by insisting that we "not overly focus on moments in time that don't reflect overarching policy."[53]

You hear that, plebeian? Don't worry about what you saw. It in no way reflected the "overarching policy" to keep a mask (or preferably, two of them) stapled to your chin.

---

51 "America remains on pause as Omicron continues," *Ipsos*, Jan. 25, 2022. https://www.ipsos.com/en-us/news-polls/axios-ipsos-coronavirus-index.

52 Crane, Emily. "Bidens seen violating DC's indoor mask mandate at pricey restaurant," *New York Post*, Oct. 18, 2021. https://nypost.com/2021/10/18/maskless-bidens-violate-dcs-indoor-mask-mandate/.

53 Psaki, Jen. White House press briefing, Oct. 18 2021. https://www.whitehouse.gov/briefing-room/press-briefings/2021/10/18/press-briefing-by-press-secretary-jen-psaki-october-18-2021/.

It would have been funny if it wasn't so depressing.

Some on the Right saw a golden opportunity for grade A mockery when Democratic Representative Alexandria Ocasio-Cortez showed up to the September 2021 annual Met Gala wearing a ridiculous white dress that said "tax the rich" on its backside.

There was nothing to laugh at or make fun of. It was simply another example of those in power, liberals running our most influential cultural and political institutions, sending a message: there's a new social hierarchy in America. And this one isn't about what you can afford to do, it's about what you're *allowed* to do.

The most important image from the dress saga wasn't the one meme-ified a million times over, wherein mini-Jenny from the Block is seen posing alone, looking back over her shoulder so the text on her dress can be seen by the camera. It's the one Ocasio-Cortez posted on Twitter, apparently being fitted for the gown. The congresswoman is not wearing a face covering. But the woman who helped her into the outfit, seen kneeling at AOC's feet, is.[54]

That's the way liberals wanted it to work. The misery of social distancing and mask wearing during the pandemic, both pushed by Democrats, the "experts," and the media, are for you, the help, to endure. Not the rich and famous. Not the ones who established and insisted on those rules. They're special. How silly of you to have thought otherwise.

Dr. Anthony Fauci had also just lectured everyday Americans about gathering outdoors—the safest place possible for avoiding infection—at sporting events. "I don't think it's smart," he had said on CNN, before dropping that timeless wisdom about strapping masks

[54] Ocasio-Cortez, Alexandria. Twitter, Sep. 14, 2021. https://twitter.com/AOC/status/1437635268664774659.

to your face, even after having gone through the trouble of being vaccinated.[55]

That was in August of 2021, which was the same month that former president Barack Obama, just a few weeks earlier, was seen on video getting amped up at an indoor birthday party with hundreds of guests and service staff in Martha's Vineyard.[56] Fauci remarkably never went on national television to address that one.

The message was clear: not all crowds are created equal. Some are better than others. Some get to break the rules that they themselves imposed.

Duke's County, where Martha's Vineyard is located, had been on an upward trend of new coronavirus infections since early July, just like almost everywhere else.[57] Why should that particular place be the exception to host a massive indoor bash without masks? Guests at the Obama party were supposedly required to have been vaccinated, but the CDC began advising face coverings for even the vaccinated when indoors a month prior.

New York Times reporter Annie Karni was sure to do her part reinforcing the new, expected social order by explaining on CNN that the Obama party attendees were "a sophisticated, vaccinated crowd."[58]

It's not enough that you did what you were told was the right thing and got vaccinated. You now have to be "sophisticated" to enjoy

---

55 Rosenstein, Mike. "Dr. Anthony Fauci has a warning for fans flocking to NFL, college football games," NJ.com, Sep. 8, 2021. https://www.nj.com/giants/2021/09/dr-anthony-fauci-has-a-warning-for-fans-flocking-to-nfl-college-football-games.html.

56 Kaminsky, Gabe. "Obama's 60th Birthday Party Is Peak Democrat COVID Sanctimony," the *Federalist*, Aug. 9, 2021. https://thefederalist.com/2021/08/09/obamas-60th-birthday-party-is-peak-democrat-covid-sanctimony.

57 "Tracking Coronavirus in Dukes County, Mass.," *New York Times*. https://www.nytimes.com/interactive/2021/us/dukes-massachusetts-covid-cases.html.

58 Kaminsky, Gabe. "Obama's Birthday Bash Safe Because It Was a 'Sophisticated, Vaccinated Crowd,'" the *Federalist*, Aug. 9, 2021. https://thefederalist.com/2021/08/09/nyt-reporter-obamas-birthday-bash-safe-because-it-was-a-sophisticated-vaccinated-crowd/.

large gatherings. And by "sophisticated," they certainly don't mean you and me.

It happened over and over. It was also in August that Democrat Representative Rashida Tlaib was seen in a video on social media, dancing at an indoor wedding in Dearborn, Michigan.[59] She wore no mask, even though cases in Wayne County, where Dearborn is located, were climbing at a quick clip.

Democratic Senator Elizabeth Warren was another one seen at yet one more indoor wedding, beaming for photos with no cover on her mouth and nose.[60] That event was in New Mexico, where the governor had put in place a universal indoor mask mandate.

It started off looking like standard political hypocrisy: Democrat Chicago Mayor Lori Lightfoot shutting down salons and then getting a handsome haircut; House Speaker Nancy Pelosi visiting a shuttered salon in San Francisco for a private, maskless primping; Democrat New York City Mayor Bill de Blasio overseeing the closure of gyms before heading to a fitness center for a quick pump; Democrat D.C. Mayor Muriel Bowser reinstating an indoor mask mandate before attending a wedding reception, inside, and without a face covering.

But when it's so frequent and with no penalty, it's no longer a matter of hypocrisy. It's the way these people believe we should live, with them doing as they wish and the rest of us following orders.

In the end, the indefinite lockdowns and the trillions in cash pumped into the economy, both so cherished by Democrats, were failures. Worse, they retarded the country in catastrophic ways.

---

59 Hroncich, Maggie. "Rep. Rashida Tlaib Pulls An Obama, Parties Maskless While Pushing Mask Mandates For The Rest Of Us," the *Federalist*, Aug. 10, 2021. https://thefederalist.com/2021/08/10/rep-rashida-tlaib-pulls-an-obama-parties-maskless-while-pushing-mask-mandates-for-the-rest-of-us/.

60 Justice, Tristan. "Elizabeth Warren Parties Maskless with Deb Haaland and Real American Indians," Aug. 30, 2021. https://thefederalist.com/2021/08/30/elizabeth-warren-parties-maskless-with-deb-haaland-and-real-american-indians/.

Scholars in Denmark and Sweden, as well as the US, concluded in a January 2022 study published by John Hopkins University that restrictions and lockdowns "had little to no effect on COVID mortality." Their best estimate was that government-imposed lockdown orders in both Europe and the US reduced COVID mortality by less than 1 percent. Specifically, restricting international travel, closing public schools and banning social gatherings had a less-than-2 percent impact on the virus death rate, according to the authors. Lockdowns, however, "imposed enormous economic and social costs where they have been adopted."[61]

Likewise, Massachusetts Institute of Technology economics professor David Autor examined payroll data of businesses that accepted loans from the government's "Paycheck Protection Program," (originally passed by President Trump and supported by Democrats and even some Republicans) and found that more than 70 percent of the programs nearly $1 trillion in funding had gone to America's top 20 percent of income earners. The program was intended for businesses to get money that would allow them to close but at the same time keep their workers on the payroll receiving checks. But in Autor's estimation, as he told the *New York Times*, "It didn't primarily go to workers who would have lost jobs. It went to business owners and their shareholders and their creditors."[62]

So much for the little guy!

Still, the condescension was never-ending. COVID vaccines were the new frontier in the Left's perpetual attempt to spread out their own anxieties and obsessions.

---

61 Herby, et al., Jonas. "A Literature Review and Meta-Analysis of the Effects of Lockdowns on COVID-19 Mortality," John Hopkins Institute for Applied Economics, Global Health, and the Study of Business Enterprise, January 2022. https://sites.krieger.jhu.edu/iae/files/2022/01/A-Literature-Review-and-Meta-Analysis-of-the-Effects-of-Lockdowns-on-COVID-19-Mortality.pdf.

62 Cowley, Stacy. "Little of the Paycheck Protection Program's $800 Billion Protected Paychecks," *New York Times*, Feb. 1, 2022. https://www.nytimes.com/2022/02/01/business/paycheck-protection-program-costs.html.

To choose to receive a vaccine for the sake of protecting yourself from severe illness should have been a completely personal decision for every individual without anyone else assuming it was his business to know what those decisions were. The CDC website made as much clear. "COVID-19 vaccines are effective at protecting you from getting sick," it said. "Based on what we know about COVID-19 vaccines, people who have been fully vaccinated can do things that they had stopped doing because of the pandemic."[63]

That's as open and shut as it gets. The vaccine is about the person who receives it and their own personal protection.

The only other consideration a person might take into account was which one of the three vaccines initially available in the US they should take. The CDC said that the two-shot dose of Pfizer was 95 percent effective at preventing infection.[64] Moderna's two-shot dose was 94.1 percent effective.[65] And Johnson & Johnson's one-shot dose was 66.3 percent effective.[66]

The most that the CDC would even say officially about receiving a shot for the sake of the health of others was that vaccination "might also help protect people around" the person who got one. "Might" being the operative word.[67]

But all Democrats and liberals in the media could do was fret over who wasn't getting a shot, insistent that they were the ones putting the vaccinated at risk.

---

63 "Stay Up to Date with Your Vaccines," CDC. https://www.cdc.gov/coronavirus/2019-ncov/vaccines/fully-vaccinated.html.

64 "Pfizer-BioNTech COVID-19 Vaccine (also known as COMIRNATY) Overview and Safety," CDC. https://www.cdc.gov/coronavirus/2019-ncov/vaccines/different-vaccines/Pfizer-BioNTech.html.

65 "Moderna COVID-19 Vaccine Overview and Safety," CDC. https://www.cdc.gov/coronavirus/2019-ncov/vaccines/different-vaccines/Moderna.html.

66 "Johnson & Johnson's Janssen COVID-19 Vaccine Overview and Safety," CDC. https://www.cdc.gov/coronavirus/2019-ncov/vaccines/different-vaccines/janssen.html

67 "COVID-19 Vaccines are Effective," CDC. https://www.cdc.gov/coronavirus/2019-ncov/vaccines/effectiveness.html.

As of this writing, nearly 80 percent of the US population had received at least one dose of a vaccine. More importantly, almost 100 percent of those in the sixty-five-years-plus range, our most vulnerable group, had at least one dose. It's not perfect, but that's the nature of a modern pandemic. Maybe the people who ended up critically ill wouldn't have been hospitalized had they been vaccinated, but that's the dice they chose to roll.

Democrats, the "experts," and the media didn't think that way. They wanted a new way to flex.

Dr. Leana Wen, a *Washington Post* contributor and CNN's chief COVID scold, became the face of vaccine nagging. Throughout 2021, she was there to serve up a steady stream of annoying lectures about why vaccination wasn't about you, but about everyone else and how it was the decent thing to do for your neighbor.

She was sort of onto something at one point, writing in the *Post* what so many others had figured out already. In mid-August of 2021 (about a year too late but better than never), she wrote that pandemic hysterics didn't have to be hopeless just because everyone won't do as they say with glee. There were options.

"It's a sad indictment of our society that children are paying the price for irresponsible adults and reckless policymakers," she said with the obligatory condescension of a COVID "expert." "As a result, parents like me who have kids too young to be vaccinated must take matters into our own hands to reduce risk."[68]

Her ideas weren't especially novel: promote the vaccination of as many adults as possible, keep a mask on, and try to stay outdoors. Most people knew about these mitigating measures already. Nonetheless, she was taking some initiative to mind her business and that was about the best we could hope for from a beloved liberal cable news "expert."

---

[68] Wen, Leana. "The pandemic has become more dangerous for children. Here's how to help keep them safe," *Washington Post*, Aug. 11, 2021. https://www.washingtonpost.com/opinions/2021/08/11/pandemic-has-become-more-dangerous-children-heres-how-help-keep-them-safe/.

And to be sure, self-reliance has always been a last resort for Democrats, if it ever comes up at all. This was one of those rare moments they had realized not everyone was interested in being told what to do, nor were they preoccupied with the affairs of people they didn't know and weren't responsible for.

For most of us, that had been the case since the beginning of the pandemic, even though, for a time, it felt like the right thing to do to be extra cautious and demonstrate a heightened sense of awareness and sensitivity. Thousands of people were dying, after all, and we weren't yet sure how this would turn out.

But since that time, we had learned a lot, like who was most susceptible to succumbing to the new coronavirus, and how to more effectively treat it. The days of deferring to the most panic-stricken control freaks had ended.

Like Wen said, everyone had the ability to "take matters into our own hands." Feel like it's safest to stay home? Stay home. Feel better in a mask? Wear as many as your capacity to breathe can handle. Comfortable with the vaccines? Get one. Get four!

Others willing to take more risks can make that decision. If the outcome is less than ideal, so be it. Some people have a lot of unprotected sex. The best anyone can do is tell them there may be severe consequences with reckless behavior. We don't tell them to walk around in public with a condom permanently affixed to their genitals. We don't demand that they avoid alcohol or dates or anything at all that might make them act on their impulses.

It's not complicated, and if all Democrats would accept what Wen had accepted for herself, they could have relaxed a little and stopped making the rest of our lives suck.

But Wen's epiphany was short-lived. With the rate of vaccinations steadily dropping as we headed into the fall of 2021, patience among "the experts" wore thin. In late August, Wen abandoned her self-reliance approach and declared that everyone should be "required" to receive a COVID vaccine, even people who had acquired antibodies against the virus from a natural infection.

"All eligible people 12 and above...would be better off getting the vaccine and should be required to do so," she wrote. "Vaccines for younger children must be an urgent priority and, once authorized, should also be mandated."[69]

That was the second paragraph of Wen's piece. She didn't even bother to build up to the prescription that we all just do whatever she says. (As an aside, that same day's issue of the *Post* had a separate column headlined, "What Dr. Leana Wen's improbable journey says about our country." It was about Wen's memoirs written about herself. It's perhaps no wonder, then, that Wen is so sure that what she has to say is important to everyone.)[70]

What followed were several paragraphs by Wen on the very scant evidence supporting a theory that receiving a vaccine dose offers better protection for individuals, even if they already have antibodies from a previous natural infection.

The one cited by Wen with the most scientific weight behind it was a report put out in the late summer of 2020 by the CDC, which Wen said "concluded that...vaccinated people have half the risk of reinfection compared with previously infected people who remained unvaccinated."

That sounds pretty authoritative, but Wen predictably excluded the important details that took the air out of her assertion. The report had actually acknowledged at the conclusion that because it was so limited in scope, "these findings cannot be used to infer causation" between a lack of vaccination of those with antibodies and the reinfection of those same individuals who did not receive a vaccine.

---

[69] Wen, Leana. "Yes, you can get some immunity from having COVID-19. But no one should wait to get vaccinated," *Washington Post*, Aug. 31, 2021. https://www.washingtonpost.com/opinions/2021/08/31/covid-19-recovery-vaccination-natural-immunity/.

[70] Tumulty, Karen. "What Dr. Leana Wen's improbable journey says about our country," *Washington Post*, Aug. 31, 2021. https://www.washingtonpost.com/opinions/2021/08/31/leana-wen-memoir-improbable-journey-public-health/.

Looking at the data reflecting a small population in Kentucky from May through June, there did seem to be a pattern showing that more unvaccinated people were reinfected with COVID than those who had also previously been infected and received a vaccine.[71] But as the author of the study acknowledged, "persons who have been vaccinated are possibly less likely to get tested," and thus, "the association of reinfection and lack of vaccination might be overestimated."

In other words, there were in all probability a lot of people who were vaccinated and reinfected but not included in the study because they didn't bother getting tested. Why would they? They had been vaccinated, the alleged purpose of which is so that the person who got a shot no longer has to think about COVID.

Drawing any conclusions from a study that relies on vaccinated folks to voluntarily get tested for COVID was stupid. It would be like counting the total number of people in a high-crime neighborhood who report seeing suspicious activity outside their homes to the police and dividing it up between those who had their doors bolted and those who had no locks at all. People with confidence that they're safe inside would understandably be less likely to call the police, but that doesn't mean something concerning didn't happen outside their homes as often as the others.

Maybe vaccinated people with antibodies really were more protected against reinfection than unvaccinated people with the same antibodies. The jury was out. To wit, the National Institutes of Health said back in March that natural antibody protection against the virus "is comparable" to the protection afforded by vaccines.[72]

What are you talking about?! Just get the vaccines! Get them all!

---

[71] Cavanaugh, Alyson et al. "Reduced Risk of Reinfection with SARS-CoV-2 After COVID-19 Vaccination—Kentucky, May–June 2021," Morbidity and Mortality Weekly Report, CDC, Aug. 13, 2021. https://www.cdc.gov/mmwr/volumes/70/wr/mm7032e1.htm.

[72] "SARS-CoV-2 antibodies protect from reinfection," National Institutes of Health, March 2, 2021. https://www.nih.gov/news-events/nih-research-matters/sars-cov-2-antibodies-protect-reinfection.

Anyway, as fate would have it, plenty of people who were vaccinated eventually were infected with the virus. According to the CDC, by the end of December of 2021, there were more than four hundred new infections each day per capita (every one hundred thousand people) among those who were vaccinated.[73] And again, that's with the reasonable presumption that vaccinated people weren't even bothering to get tested at the same rate as people who had not received any vaccine, thus depressing that number.

I have no opinion on whether people who have recovered from COVID should also receive a dose of vaccine. But if the pandemic hustlers like Wen were going to insist that doing so is necessary, they needed to do better than "Get it because I say so."

The "experts" were once again accusing the people who didn't do exactly as they demanded of putting lives at risk by simply moving through time and space.

A popular point the "experts" and certain cable news anchors liked to make when discussing vaccines was that to go unvaccinated was akin to driving while drunk. It was a clever-sounding argument, but the fact that none other than Leana Wen eventually repeated it should have been a clue that it was actually not very smart after all.

But as a mental exercise in understanding liberal stupidity, let's think the drunk driving argument through. Wen cowrote a piece in mid-September 2021 for the *Washington Post* with Sam Wang, a neuroscience professor, making the analogy.

"Some might balk at this comparison, but here are the similarities," they wrote. "Both causes of severe bodily harm are largely preventable—COVID-19 through vaccination, and drunken driving by

73 "Rates of COVID-19 Cases and Deaths by Vaccination Status," CDC. https://covid.cdc.gov/covid-data-tracker/#rates-by-vaccine-status.

not driving after drinking alcohol. Both are individual decisions with societal consequences."[74]

Fair enough. They went on to say that going unvaccinated and drunk driving are similar in that "the risk is borne not only by the person making the decision but also by others who cross their path." Additionally, they noted, even though the vaccine is not 100 percent effective in preventing severe illness or death, the more people who have it, the less transmission there is and thus the fewer deaths there are. Likewise, the more people who choose not to drive intoxicated, the safer it is for everyone on the road.

But there was a gaping hole in the analogy. Wen and Wang (don't laugh) were looking at the analogy only from the view of the person who declines to receive a vaccine or, by comparison, who drives drunkenly. Remember: We're All in This Together™ and therefore, there are other perspectives that should have also been considered when making this case. Namely, the fully vaccinated people who choose to leave their homes and, similarly, commuters who choose to drive on the road.

A person who is vaccinated, according to the "experts," had every reason to feel safe from severe illness, hospitalization, and death from COVID. As of this writing, the latest available data from the CDC showed that in December 2021, the vaccinated accounted for less than half of 1 percent of COVID-related deaths per one hundred thousand people. For the unvaccinated, it was almost ten times that amount.[75]

True, half of 1 percent isn't nothing. Some people would in fact be hospitalized or succumb fully to the virus despite having received a vaccine. With that information, a vaccinated person would have to

---

74 Wen, Leana and Wang, Sam. "Remaining unvaccinated in public should be considered as bad as drunken driving," *Washington Post*, Sep. 15, 2021. https://www.washingtonpost.com/opinions/2021/09/15/remaining-unvaccinated-public-should-be-considered-bad-drunken-driving/.

75 "Rates of COVID-19 Cases and Deaths by Vaccination Status," CDC. https://covid.cdc.gov/covid-data-tracker/#rates-by-vaccine-status.

decide whether or not he was comfortable going to a concert with hundreds of strangers or a bar indoors where other people may very well infect him. The likelihood is infinitesimal, but, sure enough, the math says he could die.

In that same vein, a person who chooses not to drink but still drive can be reasonably sure that he is safe when he puts on his seatbelt and follows the rules of the road. Odds are, though, he has seen a car accident before. He may have even experienced one that wasn't his fault. Maybe two or three of them. He can do everything right to avoid a collision, but the fact remains that other drivers are out of his control and he could become a victim of their mistakes or poor decisions.

Remove the drunk-driver factor and getting in a car still always involves a risk assessment. It's safer to drive during the day than at night. According to the National Safety Council, the vast majority of highway traffic occurs during the day and yet nighttime car accidents make up half of all accidents. A lot of that is because of visibility impairment. Inclement weather means even more risk.[76]

Plenty of people who drive and are sober get in accidents on clear days with other people who haven't been drinking at all either. It happens.

People who drive hopefully know all of this information. Yet they still determine that the odds are, if they drive cautiously, they will be okay. This is true even as drunk driving is against the law. People still drink and then get behind the wheel. We know that and we cope because we know it's not likely to happen, even though sometimes, tragically, it does.

The vaccine drama was yet another symptom of liberal misery and their anxious compulsion to tell people what to do, how to live, and how they should feel. The lecturing is endless.

---

76 "The Most Dangerous Time to Drive," National Safety Council. https://www.nsc.org/road-safety/safety-topics/night-driving.

The *New York Times* in late September 2021 ran yet another hectoring op-ed telling Americans to give up enjoying life so much because, as the author saw it, it was kind of annoying that before the pandemic, they had been.

"Americans have long had a reputation for being terrible tourists: loud, rude and too often clad in tube socks," wrote Sara Clemence.[77] "In the years leading up to the pandemic, we got even worse. Not more boisterous or more badly dressed. But—driven by cheap flights and cruises, an explosion of vacation rentals and social media-fueled FOMO [fear of missing out]—we were flooding the world, and wrecking it."

Aren't you ashamed? They so badly want you to be.

The initial months of the pandemic, of course, had people shut up in their homes, advised by the government not to step foot outside, let alone take a flight anywhere. But into the fall of 2020 and beyond, people naturally got restless and more and more began to resume travel for fun, family, and business.

That bothered antisocial liberals like Clemence, who rather enjoyed everyone's new status as shut-ins.

"Now that we are traveling again, we have a chance to usher in a better era," she wrote. "We can stop loving destinations to death. To do that, we need to travel less—and more carefully."

Are you taking notes about what you "need" to do? They never seem capable of speaking in a way that isn't offensive. "We need," "We can," "We have..." What's all this "we" talk? I don't know you. Mind your business.

Clemence offered that in addition to asking ourselves, "how to maximize our enjoyment" when traveling, we should also ask, "What impact will my presence have?" Memo to self: do not travel

---

[77] Clemence, Sara. "My Fellow Americans, Let's Be Better Tourists," *New York Times*, Sep. 29, 2021. https://www.nytimes.com/2021/09/29/opinion/americans-us-travel-tourist.html.

with Clemence or anyone else preoccupied with the "impact" their presence has.

She further advised that travelers, "Travel during the off-season" and "stay in small inns and guesthouses" wherever they go. She even included the helpful tip to "keep a close eye on any travel restrictions and recommendations from the places you want to visit" due to COVID and, plus, "make sure to comply with them fully, for your own sake and the safety of others."

(No matter how reserved or religious you are, I know that it's exceedingly difficult not to scream at these people, "Shut the hell up!" But we resist because that's the polite thing to do.)

Clemence isn't a uniquely smart or moral person. She's another liberal scold who experiences no greater joy in life than in dishing out social demerits to whomever she believes falls short of her wishes. Normal people don't care what strangers do with their lives. Liberals are always waiting in judgment.

By the way, how dare you for having expected life to resume normal programming once the worst of the pandemic was over? What, you thought all that talk about a "new normal" was a joke?

They were serious. As more Americans opted to receive a vaccine and determined that the new coronavirus was something we'd have to accept as forever part of our lives, we reengaged with the world, shopping, dining out, and traveling. Demand was surging, particularly in light of Democrats and Biden having graciously dumped another $2 trillion in new welfare dollars (otherwise known as "COVID relief money") into the economy. That was on top of the $3 trillion already pushed out by the Trump administration, bringing the country to $5 trillion that was spent to keep people out of work and in their homes. Many were making more money by doing that than they had when they held a job.

By October 2021, all of it had set us up perfectly for an inflation rate that hadn't been seen in more than thirty years. The Biden administration insisted all year that price increases on everything from gas to groceries to lumber was temporary. But by that month,

Federal Reserve Chairman Jerome Powell had said that the surge was likely to run through summer 2022.[78]

Fear not, Americans. Liberals had the answer: do less! Buy less! Come on, it'll be fun!

The Atlantic's "consumerism" columnist Amanda Mull wrote in August 2021 that the pain of out-of-stock products, delayed flights, and service industry labor shortages was not the result of supply chains breaking and Democrats having paid people for months to stay home, but the fault of consumers who were simply too comfortable expecting to get the things they want when they pay for them (preferably with a smile).

"America's ultra-tense political climate, together with the accumulated personal and economic traumas of the pandemic, have helped spur this animosity, which was already intense and common in the United States," she wrote. "But it's hardly the only reason that much of the country has decided to take out its pandemic frustrations on the customer-service desk. For generations, American shoppers have been trained to be nightmares. The pandemic has shown just how desperately the consumer class clings to the feeling of being served."[79]

Spoken like a true pissant.

You like paying for nice things? Tough! Those days are over! Now get back inside to watch Netflix all day like the rest of us.

Preaching about how everyone would need to reduce their standard of living was very en vogue among liberals who adored pandemic life.

---

78 Cox, Jeff. "Key inflation gauge watched by the Federal Reserve hits another 30-year high," CNBC.com, Oct. 1, 2021. https://www.cnbc.com/2021/10/01/key-inflation-gauge-watched-by-the-federal-reserve-hits-another-30-year-high.html.

79 Mull, Amanda. "American Shoppers Are a Nightmare," *The Atlantic*, Aug. 3, 2021. https://www.theatlantic.com/health/archive/2021/08/pandemic-american-shoppers-nightmare/619650/.

The *Washington Post* ran an op-ed in October lecturing readers not to "rant about short-staffed stores and supply chain woes."[80]

The author, Micheline Maynard, lectured that, "Rather than living constantly on the verge of throwing a fit, and risking taking it out on overwhelmed servers, struggling shop owners or late-arriving delivery people, we'd do ourselves a favor by consciously lowering expectations."

She recalled carrying a loaf of bread home from the bakery in her hands because the bakery was out of customer bags. But, she said, "I was just glad the bakery was still in business." There's that glass-half-full attitude we've come to expect from the American Left: they're just happy they could get some bread, like the good old days of the Soviet Union.

They're satisfied with that. Why aren't you?

A few days later, the news site Vox said it was "time for Americans to buy less stuff."[81] Writer Terry Nguyen asked in earnest, "When the stuff we want is so hard to get ahold of, why go to such great lengths to buy it?" The solution to product and labor shortages, he said, was simple: "We can just buy less."

And then once again in *The Atlantic*, Amanda Mull wrote under the short and sweet headline, "Stop shopping."[82] Noting the backlog of cargo ships, hundreds of which were waiting to dock and unload at understaffed ports, Mull had an idea. "[F]ew seem willing to acknowledge that the record amount of stuff being brought into the country isn't merely disappearing off store shelves," she said. "We know where

---

80 Maynard, Micheline. "Don't rant about short-staffed stores and supply chain woes," *Washington Post*, Oct. 18, 2021. https://www.washingtonpost.com/opinions/2021/10/18/dont-rant-about-short-staffed-stores-supply-chain-woes-try-lower-expectations/.

81 Nguyen, Terry. "It's time for Americans to buy less stuff," Vox.com, Nov. 22, 2021. https://www.vox.com/the-goods/22725031/buying-less-supply-chain-holiday-shopping.

82 Mull, Amanda. "Stop Shopping," *The Atlantic*, Oct. 22, 2021. https://www.theatlantic.com/technology/archive/2021/10/stop-shopping-global-supply-chain-shipping-delays/620465/.

it's going, and we know who's buying it all up. They—and maybe you—could simply knock it off."

The real problem wasn't that Joe Biden and Democrats had crushed the working spirit of Americans with obscene amounts of welfare, which in turn created record levels of inflation. It was, Mull said, that "a lot of people buy things for the sake of it, stuff they don't need or even particularly want and in many cases won't use, as a salve for boredom or anxiety or insecurity."

The projection is severe. Because liberals live in a never-ending cycle of anxiety and insecurity, they assume that's what motivates everyone else.

***

The enduring pandemic was at least good for revealing how stupid, if heartless, they can be.

There was a popular theory on the Left for why frustrating labor shortages persisted, even after those sweet federal COVID unemployment benefits dried up heading into the fall of 2021. Here's how Paul Krugman of the *New York Times* relayed that theory:

> "Well, it's only speculation, but it seems quite possible that the pandemic, by upending many Americans' lives, also caused some of them to reconsider their life choices. Not everyone can afford to quit a hated job, but a significant number of workers seem ready to accept the risk of trying something different—retiring earlier despite the monetary cost, looking for a less unpleasant job in a different industry, and so on."[83]

---

83 Krugman, Paul. "The Revolt of the American Worker," *New York Times*, Oct. 14, 2021. https://www.nytimes.com/2021/10/14/opinion/workers-quitting-wages.html.

People like Krugman believed the labor shortages were actually a good thing (he literally writes in that same piece, "Overall, it's a good thing") because they represent a sense of would-be workers being fed up with having been treated and paid poorly by employers, particularly in the service and hospitality industries.

"Long-suffering American workers, who have been underpaid and overworked for years, may have hit their breaking point," wrote Krugman, who once claimed that child pornography ended up on his computer by no fault of his own.[84]

The implication from the Left was that if you wanted the service and hospitality industries to go back to normal, greedy employers were going to have to pay their staff more and grant them better benefits. Either that, or there needed to be a significant bump in the federal minimum wage.

But the truth was that no one knew why companies and businesses were unable to hire enough people to meet the surge of consumer demand that followed the economic reopening, even as employers offered wild bonuses and pay increases. The *Times* had reported the findings of one survey that "found more than 1,600 restaurants that were paying an average wage of $13.50 plus tips across 41 states—states where earlier this year the vast majority of restaurants paid a tipped minimum wage of $5 or less."[85]

In other words, a lot of would-be workers could have been making more than double their previous earnings in the same job.

And yet, according to the Krugman theory, those jobs simply sucked so much that even an eye-popping raise couldn't reel in new workers or bring old ones back. Krugman is never right but assuming

---

84 Concha, Joe. "Paul Krugman: My computer was hacked to 'download child pornography'," the *Hill*, Jan. 9, 2020. https://thehill.com/homenews/media/477482-paul-krugman-my-computer-was-hacked-to-download-child-pornography.

85 Black, Jane. "How to Make an Unloved Job More Attractive? Restaurants Tinker with Wages," *New York Times*, Sep. 20, 2021. https://www.nytimes.com/2021/09/20/dining/restaurant-wages.html.

he was this time, his theory didn't answer for how millions of people were existing without the added federal COVID unemployment welfare and without a job income to replace it.

Were they living off of savings? Were they choosing credit card debt over a paycheck? That question was never addressed by the Krugman theory.

But, again, also assuming Krugman was right, the theory undermines two of the Left's greatest obsessions: the need for a federal minimum wage hike and the push for more cash welfare to regular people (childcare subsidies, free health insurance, universal basic income, and the like).

If all of those people, numbering in the millions, were able to walk away from these supposedly miserable jobs, even after a hefty pay increase to entice them back, while subsisting off of nothing more than their newly freed spirits, what, then, would be the point of a higher minimum wage? If they didn't want the jobs that began paying more than double what they had been by way of employers voluntarily increasing salaries, what difference would a government-mandated raise make?

And if even after the moratorium on home evictions and the additional federal unemployment benefits had lapsed, would-be workers were still just fine choosing not to work, why would yet more welfare be necessary?

The logical end to the Krugman theory was that none of it is necessary. Not then, and not now. The conclusion is that those people would rather not work and have nothing than go back to jobs they supposedly hated.

I don't know that anyone bought the idea, but if they did, they had every reason to oppose attempts by Congressional Democrats in 2021 to pass another multitrillion-dollar welfare package, which they first tried selling as "human infrastructure" and then "social spending."

They were adamant that it was needed and yet at the same time cheering on people who were simply not working at all.

Another breakthrough in stupidity was the Democrats' ridiculous "vaccine mandates work" mantra, a slogan they used to create the impression that they had been successful in governing to persuade the public to do something with their preferred outcome. But they didn't do any persuading at all. That's why they're called "mandates."

"Vaccine mandates work" was right up there with "follow the science" in mind-numbing cliche of the Left. It was repeated over and over again from the usual pandemic enthusiasts in the national media, the "experts," Biden administration officials, and so on.

Dr. Anthony Fauci, CNN, October 11: "We know that mandates work."[86]

NPR, October 7: "In the quest to get more Americans vaccinated, one thing is becoming increasingly clear: Vaccine mandates work."[87]

Washington Post, September 29: "The evidence is building: Vaccine mandates work—and well."[88]

It was probably the most sinister phrase of the pandemic era. (Other than when Jeffrey Toobin said in summer of 2021, "I didn't think other people could see me.")[89]

It was perfectly Orwellian. By "mandate," they actually meant "coercion." And by "work," they actually meant, "You really have no choice but to do as we say."

---

86 Anthony Fauci, CNN's "Situation Room with Wolf Blitzer," Oct. 11, 2021. https://www.cnn.com/2021/10/11/health/us-coronavirus-monday/index.html.

87 Hsu, Andrea. "Faced with losing their jobs, even the most hesitant are getting vaccinated," NPR.com, Oct. 7, 2021. https://www.npr.org/2021/10/07/1043332198/employer-vaccine-mandates-success-workers-get-shots-to-keep-jobs.

88 Blake, Aaron. "The evidence is building: Vaccine mandates work—and well," *Washington Post*, Sep. 29, 2021. https://www.washingtonpost.com/politics/2021/09/29/evidence-is-building-vaccine-mandates-work-well/.

89 Keveney, Bill and Puente, Maria. "Jeffrey Toobin returns as CNN legal analyst, apologizes for exposing himself on Zoom call," *USA Today*, June 10, 2021. https://www.usatoday.com/story/entertainment/tv/2021/06/10/jeffrey-toobin-apologizes-transgression-zoom-cnn-return/7641703002/.

Some virus lovers were arguing that, no, in fact, everyone had a choice. They could choose to receive a vaccine—they were free!—or you could find a new life. That was the ultimatum that President Biden was issuing with glee, ordering healthcare providers, full-time federal workers, and government contractors to get injected or lose their livelihoods.

On the horizon at the time was an order for private companies with more than one hundred employees to also institute COVID vaccine mandates. If workers hadn't gotten a shot in a number of days, employers would face penalties that could reach into the hundreds of thousands of dollars, which naturally meant that those who chose not to load up on vaccines were all but certain to be cut for costing the company.

So, those were the options. Get a vaccine or give up your income.

Some companies, like major airlines, had gotten ahead of the government and began mandating that their employees get a shot, which did lead to a surge of new vaccinations. What else would be expected? Of course most people would rather keep their income than watch their financial savings slip away while at the same time panicking about the obscene levels of inflation of the time.

Every indication is that the vaccines were safe and effective in reducing severe illness. But plenty of people had legitimate reasons for deciding it wasn't for them, whether it was because they had already developed antibodies from natural COVID infection or because they would have felt more comfortable with more time, among other reasons.

That freedom was enthusiastically snatched from them by control freaks (liberals) in the government and the media, high on their own supply of Moderna. They were all very chipper as they repeated the creepy line that "vaccine mandates work," but it was only more dishonesty. If they were sincere about any of it, they would have called a vaccine "mandate" what it really was: coercion.

It's hard to believe that Biden had once unequivocally said he was opposed to a government vaccine mandate. "No, I don't think it should be mandatory," he said in December 2020. "I wouldn't demand it be mandatory…just like I don't think masks have to be made mandatory nationwide."[90] By October 2021, Biden was a mandate hype man, confounded that anyone wouldn't want a shot.

"Let's be clear," he said that month in remarks about the mandates his administration was pushing with zeal, "vaccination requirements should not be another issue that divides us."[91]

Yes, he actually said that forcing people to inject their bodies with a drug shouldn't be controversial. It turned out to be very divisive. The Supreme Court would eventually rule in January 2022 that the mandate on large private companies for their workers to either be vaccinated or be frequently tested exceeded the administration's authority.[92] And a district judge in Texas blocked a separate mandate issued by Biden that required all federal employees to receive a vaccine (with no testing option allowed).[93]

All the while, the media remained fixated on Republican Florida Governor Ron DeSantis. But funny enough, they only talked about him if they could link a rise of infections in that state to his aversion to restrictions, masks, and mandates, otherwise ignorantly referred to by liberals as "The Science."

In a normal world, to "follow the science" would mean to survey all available data, process the latest information, and then make decisions in line based on an educated conclusion. But we weren't living in

---

90 "Biden: 'I don't think Covid vaccine should be mandatory," BBC, Dec. 4, 2020. https://www.bbc.com/news/av/world-us-canada-55195831.

91 Biden, Joe. Remarks at the White House, Oct. 14, 2021. https://www.whitehouse.gov/briefing-room/speeches-remarks/2021/10/14/remarks-by-president-biden-on-the-covid-19-response-and-vaccination-program-2/.

92 Liptak, Adam. "Supreme Court Blocks Biden's Virus Mandate for Large Employers," *New York Times*, Jan. 13, 2022. https://www.nytimes.com/2022/01/13/us/politics/supreme-court-biden-vaccine-mandate.html.

93 Hassan, Adeel. "A U.S. judge blocks Biden's vaccine mandate for federal workers, months after most were vaccinated," *New York Times*, Jan. 21, 2022. https://www.nytimes.com/live/2022/01/21/world/omicron-covid-vaccine-tests#a-us-judge-blocks-bidens-vaccine-mandate-for-federal-workers-months-after-most-were-vaccinated.

a normal world. We were living in a state of media-generated hysteria where "follow the science" meant shutting down everything, strapping a mask (preferably two) on your face, and behaving as though every move you make might result in sudden death.

Throughout the summer of 2021, Florida and much of the Southeast finally went through what other parts of the country had already experienced—[94]an intense wave of infections that naturally meant a surge in the number of COVID-related hospitalizations and, sadly, deaths. Virtually every state, at some point, went through this at least once, if not twice. New York, New Jersey, and a lot of the Northeast got it first. Then the Midwest. Then it was Florida's turn, peaking at an average of nearly thirty thousand new cases per day in mid-August.

Because DeSantis opposed mask requirements in public schools and vaccine mandates for private businesses while at the same time enjoying a beer in public, the media attributed the wash of cases directly to the governor.

Jennifer Rubin of the *Washington Post* accused DeSantis of being one of the "right-wing politicians who have formed a sort of death cult."[95]

Vanity Fair called him the "angel of death."[96]

Charles Blow in the *New York Times* said that by resisting the Left's beloved economic restrictions and mask mandates, DeSantis

---

94 Hassan, Adeel. "A U.S. judge blocks Biden's vaccine mandate for federal workers, months after most were vaccinated," *New York Times*, Jan. 21, 2022. https://www.nytimes.com/live/2022/01/21/world/omicron-covid-vaccine-tests#a-us-judge-blocks-bidens-vaccine-mandate-for-federal-workers-months-after-most-were-vaccinated.

95 Rubin, Jennifer. "Even businesses are trying to thwart the Republican death cult," *Washington Post*, Aug. 2, 2021. https://www.washingtonpost.com/opinions/2021/08/02/businesses-try-thwart-republicans-death-cult/.

96 Levin, Bess. "Ron DeSantis, Angel of Death: Parents Can Still Send Kids to School After Exposure to COVID-19," *Vanity Fair*, Sep 23, 2021. https://www.vanityfair.com/news/2021/09/ron-desantis-schools-coronavirus-exposure.

was allowing Floridians "to choose death so that he can have a greater political life."[97]

The Left had spent the entire past year politicizing the pandemic in obvious ways, but nothing ever quite revealed their motives as much as when they chose to pay attention to Florida. By the fall, though, there was a Florida national news blackout, and it wasn't a mystery why. The numbers explained it.

The tables had turned.

At the tail end of October 2021, the only state beating Florida for the lowest number of average daily new infections was Hawaii. By October 27, Florida had even beat Hawaii. And that was despite plenty of other blue states having a higher rate of vaccination against COVID than did Florida.

On October 19, Florida was averaging eleven new infections for every one hundred thousand people per day. By contrast, New York, which has close to the same population size (Florida has a slightly higher one), was averaging more than double that. At the time, 59 percent of Florida's population was "fully vaccinated." In New York, it was seven points higher.[98]

That was a lot of spread in New York but no one was accusing the state's Democrat Governor Kathy Hochul of being an "angel of death." The politics of COVID are apparently less interesting when the Left was unable to find fault in DeSantis and when it was Democrat leaders whose states were floundering.

To be fair, which liberals never are, that was only taking into account a certain segment of time. If we had to look at data that expanded the entire pandemic up until then—well, actually, we'd still see that Florida had not been the morgue that Democrats kept claiming it was.

---

97 Blow, Charles. "Ron DeSantis, How Many Covid Deaths Are Enough?" *New York Times*, Aug. 29, 2021. https://www.nytimes.com/2021/08/29/opinion/ron-desantis-covid-death.html.

98 "Coronavirus in the U.S.: Latest Map and Case Count," *New York Times*. https://www.nytimes.com/interactive/2021/us/covid-cases.html.

Stipulating that the most important measure of success in managing a public health crisis is in keeping people alive, death rates in the top ten states at the time didn't reflect any pattern related to partisan politics at all. Mississippi, a red state, had the highest death rate with 335 deaths per one hundred thousand people. Blue New Jersey was second, with 313. Alabama and Louisiana, two red states, followed. And then New York, a blue state, came in at number five for all-time highest death rate. Florida, under DeSantis, was in ninth place.[99]

Multiple other red states had a higher death rate than Florida, but you probably never even heard the names of those governors. Of course not. Florida is a crucial swing state in presidential elections, and DeSantis was a nationally popular Republican who obviously wanted to run for the White House in 2024. His pestering critics in the media knew what they were doing.

***

The chaos of COVID was great for Democrats in the 2020 election. It was their excuse to throw out all the rules that keep voting transparent and legitimate. Deadlines on mail-in ballots? Gone, it's a pandemic. Limits on who can vote absentee? Gone, it's a pandemic. Regulations on early voting? Gone, it's a pandemic.

The result was an absolute, unaccountable mess of ballots that gushed into the voting centers of major counties in critical states like Pennsylvania, Georgia, Arizona, and Wisconsin, with envelopes turning up in random boxes, nooks, crannies, and anywhere else that "voter rights" groups could think of.

In late November, weeks after Election Day in 2020, nearly four hundred uncounted ballots manifested in Democrat-leaning Milwaukee.[100]

---

99 Ibid.

100 Calvi, Jason and Bauer, Scott. "Nearly 400 uncounted ballots found in Wisconsin recount," Fox6 Milwaukee, Nov. 24, 2020. https://www.fox6now.com/news/nearly-400-uncounted-ballots-found-in-wisconsin-recount.

A judge in Georgia ordered the unsealing of nearly one hundred fifty thousand absentee ballots in Georgia, months after the 2020 election.[101]

Officials in Philadelphia had tens of thousands of ballots remaining to count more than twenty-four hours after Election Day but wouldn't offer a deadline as to when the counting would be done.[102]

Those episodes took place everywhere, over and over again, with new ballots "discovered" or "waiting to be counted" (always to the benefit of Joe Biden). And the courts allowed all of it, regardless of state laws that had been put in place to prevent such a thing.

Well, what do you expect? It was a pandemic!

Donald Trump maintains that he was robbed of reelection in large part because of the confusion caused by the delayed ballot counting and snap rulings from courts against election regulations that were written into law.

Liberals pretend that his complaints are an affront to decency and a threat to democracy, as if they themselves don't do the same thing all the time. Even before the 2020 election, they were publicly doubting its legitimacy.

Democrats swear they're the ones upholding all of American democracy while former President Trump spends his days molesting "the norms," and yet all they could do was sow doubt about the outcome of 2020.

---

[101] Reimann, Nicholas. "Georgia Set For Another Election Audit After Judge Unseals 145,000 Absentee Ballots," *Forbes*, May 21, 2021. https://www.forbes.com/sites/nicholasreimann/2021/05/21/georgia-set-for-another-election-audit-after-judge-unseals-145000-absentee-ballots/?sh=8150f46f5ec5.

[102] Moselle, Aaron, et al. "Pa. Election 2020 Results: Philly closer to finishing count of mail ballots; at PHL, Trump campaign claims victory," Whyy.org, Nov. 4, 2020. https://whyy.org/articles/pa-election-2020-results-thousands-of-philly-mail-ballots-still-left-to-count/.

In the span of just five minutes on CNN one day in August that year, three of them said the only way Trump could secure victory in November was if he stole it.[103]

"This man is not going to win fairly. So why are we supporting crooked activity?"—Democratic Representative Jim Clyburn of South Carolina (to which the anchor seriously replied, "I feel your passion").

"The only way he feels now he can win this against the Biden-Harris ticket is to straight out steal it, and he's doing it in plain sight, and we cannot let it happen."—Democrat former Senator Barbara Boxer of California.

"Whether it is suppressing the vote by instilling fear in people that vote by mail or whether it's little back-of-the-room meetings between Kanye and his consigliere Jared Kushner, he's going to find every single way he can to steal this election, to rig this election in his favor."—CNN liberal commentator Ana Navarro.

It was worth a million fact-checks from the media anytime Trump claimed that universal mail-in voting would lead to significant fraud, but there wasn't so much as a peep when Democrats stated out loud that the election would be illegitimate unless their candidate won. The best they can muster is, "I feel your passion."

So much for all that "undermining the integrity of our democracy" talk.

It was apparently Trump's great scheme to fix the November election by—wait for it—slowing down the mail![104] Admittedly, it was a diabolical plan only slightly more impressive than the Democrats' effort to defeat Trump by advocating for a never-ending economic shutdown in response to a virus that is largely harmless to most of us, but they did what they could.

---

[103] CNN's "Newsroom," Aug. 15, 2020. http://edition.cnn.com/TRANSCRIPTS/2008/15/cnr.08.html.

[104] York, Byron. "A reality-based look at Trump and the post office," *Washington Examiner*, Aug. 16, 2020. https://www.washingtonexaminer.com/opinion/columnists/a-reality-based-look-at-trump-and-the-post-office.

But the problem with the charge that Trump was tinkering with the post office in order to rig the election, in addition to being untrue, was that slowing down the rate at which votes were counted didn't mean they wouldn't be. So long as a mail-in vote was postmarked by the proper deadline, it was supposed to be tallied. (Not that "deadlines" really mattered. It was a pandemic!)

Like most people who've heard of the internet, Democrats never seriously had a burning passion for the post office. If they did, it wouldn't bleed money year after year. If anything, it looks like they were trying to sabotage it further that year by refusing to flush more money into it with a stand-alone bill, which the Trump White House had said it was willing to negotiate. (Instead, Democrats were trying to pass funding for the postal service in a bigger economic relief package, which had more and more welfare that Republicans weren't so keen on.)

The Left's professed commitment to faith in our elections is just like everything else they do—it's a cynical act intended to disguise their depraved pursuits of power as anxious concern for the health of our democracy.

It only matters when they think it benefits them politically and the pandemic benefited them greatly.

How could they give it up?

Lucky for them, they didn't have to. By mid-January of 2022, the daily average of new infections had soared more than three times what they had been at their peak under Trump. In just one year with Democrats in charge of Congress and the White House, the virus spread wider and faster than ever before. Hospitalizations had also surpassed what we had seen under Trump.[105]

We even got the bonus of having the most highly contagious variant yet, Omicron, born under Biden's watch.

---

105 "Coronavirus in the U.S.: Latest Map and Case Count," *New York Times*. https://www.nytimes.com/interactive/2021/us/covid-cases.html.

If Democrats and the "public health experts" were capable of shame, they all would have resigned from their posts to pursue a life of ice fishing in obscurity. But they aren't.

Biden, the one who promised to "shut down" the pandemic, instead threw up his hands to let us know it's not his problem. "Look, there is no federal solution," Biden declared from the White House at the end of 2021. "This gets solved at a state level."[106]

Joe Biden on October 15, 2020: "We're eight months into this pandemic, and Donald Trump still doesn't have a plan to get this virus under control. I do."[107]

Biden fourteen months later: "Look, there is no federal solution."

Fauci, referred to by some as "Nerd Jesus," said two weeks later with resignation that "just about everybody" would be infected by the new variant.[108]

Oh, but don't mistake any of that as admission that the people in charge had no clue what they were doing, were helpless in limiting the spread of the virus (as they said they could) or were taking a backseat to anyone who might dare to let up on their beloved mandates and restrictions. No, no, so long as liberals had the power, those were here to stay, to be turned on and off as they please, despite not having done anything to change the course of the pandemic from bad to worse.

Liberals loved everything about the pandemic. They loved politicizing it. They loved using it as a license to tell people what to do. They loved having it as a reason to push for more welfare spending. They loved that it could be cited to further their agendas on virtually

---

106 Biden, Joe. Remarks at the White House, Dec. 27, 2021. https://www.whitehouse.gov/briefing-room/speeches-remarks/2021/12/27/remarks-by-president-biden-at-covid-19-response-teams-regular-call-with-the-national-governors-association/.

107 Biden, Joe. Twitter, Oct. 15, 2020. https://twitter.com/joebiden/status/1316894374500962305?lang=en.

108 Jeong, Andrew, et al. "Virus may infect most, Fauci says, but risk of severe illness 'very, very low' for vaccinated," *Washington Post*, Jan. 12, 2022. https://www.washingtonpost.com/nation/2022/01/12/covid-omicron-variant-live-updates/.

everything, from election tampering to climate change and even to increasing the minimum wage.

They had success with the virus by doing what they do best—spread misery.

3

Spot the White Supremacist (Hint: He's Black)

Racial tension and liberals go hand in glove. I'm convinced that without one, the other wouldn't even exist. Much of it is attributable to the Leftists in the media who never tire of a good race war.

And both 2020 and 2021 had been nothing if not one long, ongoing race war. So wedded are liberals to race drama that they literally create it where it doesn't exist.

The Kyle Rittenhouse verdict is proof positive of the Left's racial neurosis and the need to bring down everyone with it.

In November 2021, Rittenhouse was acquitted of three homicide charges (among other offenses) stemming from the BLM riots in Kenosha, Wisconsin, during the previous summer.

Rittenhouse was seventeen at the time when he went into Kenosha with a medic kit and a loaded AR-15 with a friend for the purpose of protecting a small car dealership from any further damage that might be caused by rioters. The business owners had already seen extensive damage to their property from days of riots, which ignited after police shot Jacob Blake, a twenty-nine-year-old black man, who was accused of violating a restraining order after sexually assaulting a woman. She claimed Blake touched her genitals, put his fingers to his nose, and said, "Smells like you've been with other men," according to the *New York Post*.[109]

I wasn't there and don't know if it happened, but that's why police were pursuing him, and video footage showed that Blake was non-compliant with cops when they attempted to arrest him. He instead ventured to his car, opened the door to do who knows what. That's when he was shot.

Blake was, decidedly, no angel.[110] But despite not knowing really anything at the time about his run-in with the police, liberals, high off their previous destruction that year related to the death of George Floyd, once again took to the streets in Kenosha to wreak havoc. The city ultimately would endure $50 million in damage to public and private property.[111] At least forty businesses closed permanently. The Kenosha County supervisor called the riots "the biggest crisis in the history" of the city.

Sheriff David Beth recalled the mayhem, telling the *New York Times* a year after, "It happened so quickly. We did not anticipate them lighting small mom-and-pop businesses on fire. And we didn't have the manpower to go protect everything as we would have liked to."[112]

---

109 Fonrouge, Gabrielle. "This is why Jacob Blake had a warrant out for his arrest," *New York Post*, Aug. 28, 2020. https://nypost.com/2020/08/28/this-is-why-jacob-blake-had-a-warrant-out-for-his-arrest/.

110 "Michael Brown 'no angel' controversy," BBC.com, Aug. 25, 2014. https://www.bbc.com/news/blogs-echochambers-28929087.

111 Flores, Terry. "Damage due to rioting, unrest in Kenosha tops $50 million; 2,000 Guard assisted here," *Kenosha News*, Sep. 9, 2020. https://www.kenoshanews.com/news/local/damage-due-to-rioting-unrest-in-kenosha-tops-50-million-2-000-guard-assisted-here/article_26473ec9-c08a-5490-9d09-cc2b840b65f1.html.

112 Bosman, Julie. "A Year After Unrest, a Scarred Kenosha Still Waits to Rebuild," *New York Times*, Sep. 14, 2021. https://www.nytimes.com/2021/09/14/us/kenosha-wisconsin-jacob-blake.html?.?mc=aud_dev&ad-keywords=auddevgate&gclid=Cj0KCQjwlOmLBhCHARIsAGiJg7nQPrYjZVE9t0ck9WYwLZ7dIalpFqOrh5Zt5EBiQwlS_ga0VICQfZEaAiPbEALw_wcB&gclsrc=aw.ds.

That's why Rittenhouse was there that night. It wasn't because of Blake or that black protesters were demonstrating against police brutality. It was because of the rioting in a city where he had family and where he worked as a recreation pool lifeguard.

Unfortunately for Rittenhouse, the presence of armed men who opposed the anarchy was not welcome. He would find himself chased into a car lot and cornered by a raving lunatic with an extended history of sexual offenses, including the anal rape of children.[113] Joseph Rosenbaum, a man in his mid-thirties, was partaking in the rioting that night, lighting fires and taunting those who were trying to protect businesses from further damage. In one video from the scene, Rosenbaum is viewed repeatedly shouting, "Shoot me, nigga!"[114]

During the trial, witnesses testified that Rosenbaum had made direct threats to others, including Rittenhouse, saying he would "kill you mother fuckers," "mother fucking niggers"[115] and that he would "cut your fucking hearts out and kill you."[116]

By contrast, Rittenhouse was only ever recorded on video explaining that he was on scene to protect the car lot and to offer medical aid to anyone who needed it. He was seen calling out, "Medical, medical, medical" and "friendly, friendly, friendly" to let others know he wasn't hostile.

But it was he who would end up alone in the dark hours, strolling by a parking lot, when Rosenbaum emerged from between the shadows of four cars. A separate rioter yelled, "Get him!" and Rosenbaum began to give chase. Rittenhouse attempted to run away and even

---

113 Piwowarczyk, Jim. "Joseph Rosenbaum: Sex Offender 2002 Arizona Criminal Complaint," Wisconsin Right Now, March 11, 2021. https://www.wisconsinrightnow.com/2021/03/11/joseph-rosenbaum-sex-offender/.

114 "Joseph Rosenbaum: "Shoot me, nigga!" at Kenosha riot, Aug 26, 2020," YouTube.com, Nov. 9, 2021. https://www.youtube.com/watch?v=t8kgAAeSpDo.

115 Gouveia, Robert F. Twitter, Nov. 20, 2021 https://twitter.com/RobertGrulerEsq/status/1462259539877797888.

116 Richmond, Todd. "A look at key points in Kyle Rittenhouse's testimony," *Associated Press*, Nov. 10, 2021. https://apnews.com/article/kyle-rittenhouse-trial-key-points-bc51f3b9dd0fe0c1289fe2161d7c3ab3.

turned back once to wield his weapon as a warning but Rosenbaum continued to advance. The gap was closing and when Rittenhouse found himself wedged between parked cars and a building, he once again turned to face his pursuer. This time, he fired four shots. An independent eye-witness testified that Rosenbaum had been reaching for Rittenhouse's gun when he was pumped full of bullets.

Immediately after his fatal encounter with Rosenbaum, Rittenhouse began heading toward the police to alert them about the incident. As he jogged, a mob began to form behind him. Another person, Gaige Grosskreutz, in his mid-twenties, attempted to talk to Rittenhouse as he made his way but others in the mob began shouting, "He just shot him!" and, "Get his ass!"

Rittenhouse picked up his pace in the direction of police as the mob advanced. Eventually, it caught up with him. A man swung at Rittenhouse's head, which knocked the teen's baseball cap off of his head. He tried continuing forward but tripped and tumbled to the ground with his gun.

Video then shows a man—identified in court only as "jump kick man"—hopping into the air and slamming his boot into Rittenhouse's face. Another man, identified as Anthony Huber, makes an attempt at striking Rittenhouse across the head with his skateboard. Huber then advanced once again on Rittenhouse, who fired his gun at him, hitting him in the chest. At that moment, Grosskreutz was moving in on Rittenhouse, who was still on the ground, seated upright in an effort to regain his footing. Rittenhouse wielded his weapon, and Grosskreutz, who was armed with his own Glock, put his hands up. But as Rittenhouse went to lift himself up off the ground, video shows Grosskreutz advancing on Rittenhouse with his gun pointed in the direction of Kyle's face. Rittenhouse fired his gun once again, blowing off Grosskreutz's right bicep.

Finally having received the message that this guy wasn't afraid to fire his weapon at a threat, the mob withdrew and Rittenhouse continued his way, hands up, to police. He was sprayed with chemical irritant and told to go home, with police testifying during the trial that they didn't further engage him as a suspect because they could hear yet more gunfire and believed there remained an active shooter beyond.

Two of the men that Rittenhouse shot that night died. One survived. Most crucially, all three were white. And other than Rosenbaum—the first person Rittenhouse shot and who was seen yelling the n-word—there is no evidence that anyone involved had said anything that night regarding race.

You would think that because he was using the n-word so brazenly, a sizable portion of blacks would believe Rosenbaum had it coming. Rittenhouse would have been heralded as a legend among blacks, if not for the media's slanderous narrative that he was a white supremacist, out of line for being in a place he had every right to be.

But watching MSNBC's Joy Reid, you'd have been under the impression the Rittenhouse saga was about the lynching of a blameless black man.

A few days in advance of the trial, Reid pondered whether there was anything prosecutors could do to "make sure that this doesn't wind up being a jury that essentially approximates the Emmet Till jury back in the 1950s."

Her guest Paul Butler, a law professor at Georgetown, advanced the race-baiting, declaring that an acquittal of Rittenhouse "would be a call to arms for anyone who wants to police a Black Lives Matter march," which would send the message that "badges are no longer required for self-appointed law enforcement officers at Black Lives Matter protests."[117]

Butler added, "If a 17-year-old kid who shot three people with a gun he's not even supposed to have can get away with this then anybody can, who wants to attack a protest. Well, at least anybody white."

---

[117] Scarry, Eddie. "The Media Need A Kyle Rittenhouse Conviction in Order to Validate Leftist Political Violence," the *Federalist*, Oct. 28, 2021. https://thefederalist.com/2021/10/28/the-media-need-a-kyle-rittenhouse-conviction-in-order-to-validate-leftist-political-violence/.

It's a theme that persisted all the way to the end. As the trial wrapped up and the jury broke for deliberation, *New York Times* columnist Farhad Manjoo recalled Rittenhouse as "the white teenager who shot and killed two people and injured a third during a night of Black Lives Matter protests and civil unrest in Kenosha, Wis., last year." Manjoo believed the race of the shooter was worth mentioning—"the white teenager"!—but apparently thought that demographic detail was uninteresting when it came to the men who were shot. Readers just needed to know that these men were at "a night of Black Lives Matter protests and civil unrest."

What person wouldn't come away with anything other than a sense that Rittenhouse had shot some black people?

When the rest of the public began to realize that no one involved in this case was black, liberals still attempted to explain that bothersome fact away.

An article in *Politico* headlined, "The Rittenhouse Trial Is All about Race," said, "The issue of race, of course, is linchpin to it all" because "even though Rittenhouse, who is white, is accused of killing two white men…[h]e's been lionized by opponents of the Black Lives Matter movement."[118]

It's a wonder more journalists don't suffer from severed spinal cords with the way they contort themselves to make a point about race that isn't there.

After the not-guilty verdict had been rendered, Paul Butler wrote in the *Washington Post* that, "Regardless of whether Rittenhouse wants or deserves to be, he is now the poster child for reactionary White men who seek to take the law in their own hands, who want to patrol Black Lives Matter protests with assault weapons and who think that violence is a legitimate form of political discourse."

---

[118] Booker, Brakkton. "The Rittenhouse trial is all about race," *Politico*, Nov. 16, 2021. https://www.politico.com/newsletters/the-recast/2021/11/16/kyle-rittenhouse-trial-race-gun-shooting-kenosha-495121.

Post columnist Eugene Robinson similarly wrote, "[S]ince the Kenosha protest was about racial justice and police violence against Black Americans, race was very much the subtext of the Rittenhouse trial, too. Rittenhouse became seen as an avatar of White grievance and anger."[119]

By "became seen," Robinson means he and other liberals decided race was involved even though it was expressly not involved. To the Right, Rittenhouse was nothing more than a sign that not everyone was okay with lawless rioting, that there were good people willing to help maintain order when police were outnumbered and told by elected Democrats to stand down.

The answer as to why, then, the angry Left was so invested in this case is easy. They wanted a conviction that would then justify the rioting as a legitimate form of political violence, plus further cement Black Lives Matter and its supporters as a dominant, national force—a force that uses violence for votes, which is the exact opposite of "democracy," but a force nonetheless.

What's the best way to achieve political compliance in America? By turning well-meaning people so exhausted, so fed up, so resigned that they'll do whatever you say. That was the Left's strategy all through the Trump years, and it remains the strategy today.

The irony of the alliance between BLM and Democrats is that liberals are hyper-prejudiced when it comes to race. Anyone can see it and all it takes is to literally let liberals speak.

Scholars from two prestigious universities released a study in 2018 demonstrating the tendency of White liberals to dumb down their speech when communicating with Blacks. In their paper titled "The Competence Downshift by White Liberals," professors Cydney Dupree at Yale and Susan Fiske of Princeton argued that Whites on the Left "self-present less competence to minorities than to other

---

[119] Robinson, Eugene. "Kyle Rittenhouse's not-guilty verdict should not be a green light for other armed vigilantes," *Washington Post*, Nov. 19, 2021. https://www.washingtonpost.com/opinions/2021/11/19/kyle-rittenhouse-not-guilty-verdict-must-not-encourage-armed-vigilantes/.

Whites." In other words, "they patronize minorities stereotyped as lower status and less competent" in their speech.[120]

The paper said that "liberals—but not conservatives—presented less competence to Black interaction partners than to White ones." The conclusion was not that liberals deliberately condescend to Blacks. But that, "with the best of intentions—seeking to affiliate with a Black interaction partner—White liberals may unwittingly draw on negative stereotypes, dumbing themselves down in a likely well-meaning, 'folksy,' but ultimately patronizing, attempt to connect with the" Black counterpart.

You've probably seen this take place in real life. A goofy White liberal with no sense of style or rhythm encounters a Black person or group of Blacks and suddenly decides it's time to jive, adopting an unrecognizable affect, vocabulary, and accent. The cringe factor is severe, and the study's authors argued that such an incident is far more common when the White person happens to be on the political Left.

To wit, the authors said that in an effort to meet the expectations of Blacks, who liberals view through a lens of negative stereotypes, "Getting along with a lower-status group may entail presenting oneself as less competent or lower in status—that is, 'getting down with the people.'"

The study drew these conclusions based on public remarks by White Democrat and Republican leaders in front of various audiences, and word choice of self-identified White liberals versus White conservatives when encountered with another person, either White or Black.

In the case of analyzing public speeches and remarks by party leaders, Democrats "expressed significantly less competence—using fewer words related to power and agency—to minority audiences than to White audiences."

---

[120] Dupree, C. H., and Fiske, S. T. (in press). "Self-Presentation in Interracial Settings: The Competence Downshift by White Liberals," *Journal of Personality and Social Psychology*, 2018. https://psyarxiv.com/pv2ab/.

In another experiment, university-level students were given a hypothetical scenario wherein they were part of a book club and tasked with offering their thoughts on the latest literature and submitting them in an email to the club secretary. Some students were told the secretary was named "Emily" and others were told she was named "Lakisha."

Participants were then asked to choose from a list of words that they would use in such a scenario to describe the assigned book. The terms had a range of sophistication. For example, a student could choose between "euphoric" and "happy" to convey positivity, or between "melancholy" or "sad" to convey negative emotion.)

The results were the same. "[L]iberal participants engaged in a competence downshift, selecting words that would make them appear significantly less competent with a Black interaction partner than with a White one," the authors wrote. "Conservative participants, in contrast, engaged in no such competence downshift, selecting words that would make them appear equally competent with a Black or White partner."

To be fair, the study also theorized that the reason white conservatives don't do the same thing is simply because they are not trying to draw common ground with minorities, thus declining to modulate the way they communicate. But that doesn't account for why liberals would choose to feed into negative stereotypes about blacks in order to have a more favorable interaction. That can only be explained by acknowledging that those on the political Left tend to have an inherent prejudice that is not shared by the Right.

No matter what way you cut it, it's a bigotry that liberals harbor. How do they get away with it? Why, by blaming white supremacy, of course!

Even when minorities do something demonstrably wrong, there's a white person somewhere for liberals to blame.

Charles Blow, the *New York Times*'s perpetual columnist-in-training, wrote in August 2021 on a spate of prominent black men who at the time had mocked, belittled, and disparaged other black men who are gay.

"Let me say first that the country has quickly evolved on the acceptance of gayness, and that includes an evolution among Black people," he said. "But, as acceptance and visibility rise, the minority who feel threatened by gay people has grown louder. They talk in apocalyptic terms about a 'gay agenda' destined to recruit throngs to a gay 'lifestyle.'"[121]

The minority of blacks who "feel threatened by gay people has grown louder," you say? Why, that sounds awful and like something black people may want to work out among themselves!

But that's where the social justice, "critical race" nonsense comes in. According to liberals, even the bigotries, prejudices, and patterns of antisocial behavior exhibited by ethnic minorities can all be traced back to the ultimate evil—whiteness.

Blow went on to say that black people who oppress other black people for being gay are actually doing so because of white supremacy. "In a society that treats racism as a sport," he continued, "in which each racial group is jockeying against the others, all of them shadowed by a culture of white supremacy laced with misogyny, anything that reduces your percentage of straight males, or 'feminizes' them, is seen as weakening the race."

Black homophobes are "doing the work of the white supremacist patriarchy," Blow said.

If you understood none of that, it's because it has no foundation in logic or critical thinking (which are in and of themselves tools of white supremacy, they say).[122] No, it's simply more excuse-making for a tendency that is, even according to liberal institutions, particularly prevalent in a specific nonwhite race.

---

[121] Blow, Charles. "The Anti-Gay Agenda," *New York Times*, Aug. 25, 2021. https://www.nytimes.com/2021/08/25/opinion/homophobia-lgbt-hip-hop.html.

[122] York, Byron. Twitter, July 15, 2020. https://twitter.com/ByronYork/status/1283372233730203651.

The CDC's website—a religious text of the Left—addresses it outright. A page on "HIV and African American People" states that "Black/African American people account for a higher proportion of new HIV diagnoses and people with HIV, compared to other races and ethnicities." In 2018, blacks made up 13 percent of the population but shockingly accounted for just shy of half of the total new HIV infections that year.[123] The site lists the "challenges" black communities have in preventing infection. One of them is homophobia, which "can make it difficult for some African American people to be open about risk-taking behaviors."

In other words, homophobia among black people results in a lot of black people contracting HIV because men feel pressured into keeping their homosexuality a secret, and thus pass the virus on to unsuspecting women, who in turn pass it on during pregnancy.

CNN's formerly sane Don Lemon said in 2011, "I think there is a segment of the black community—a big segment of the black community—that are homophobic and it has a lot to do with religion." He said that "In black culture, and similar in Latino and other minority cultures, it's the worst thing you can do as a man."[124]

Homophobia as an issue among Black people is so well known that a 2017 headline at the Black-centric news website The Root blared the words to its 90 percent black audience (the other 10 percent are young white men who look like Rachel Maddow): "Stop Pretending to Be Shocked at Homophobia in the Black Community."[125]

But white supremacy!

Liberals can find it anywhere. And by "find it," I of course mean "make it up out of nowhere."

---

[123] "HIV and African American People," CDC. https://www.cdc.gov/hiv/group/racialethnic/africanamericans/index.html.

[124] "Don Lemon: Yes, the Black Community Is Homophobic," TheRoot.com, May 17, 2011. https://www.theroot.com/don-lemon-yes-the-black-community-is-homophobic-1790863975.

[125] Harriot, Michael. "Stop Pretending to Be Shocked at Homophobia in the Black Community,"TheRoot.com, Feb. 11, 2017. https://www.theroot.com/stop-pretending-to-be-shocked-at-homophobia-in-the-blac-1792228332.

Former President Trump, to the dismay of Democrats, was known to have a certain appeal among nonwhite men. And when many of those nonwhite men showed up to support him at the January 6 "Stop the Steal" rally, the *Washington Post* reacted by running an op-ed explaining it away as—get this—racism.

"I call this phenomenon multiracial whiteness—the promise that they, too, can lay claim to the politics of aggression, exclusion and domination," wrote the author, New York University Professor Cristina Beltrán. She explained her comical theory, wherein people who aren't white strive to be white, as based in "an ideology invested in the unequal distribution of land, wealth, power and privilege—a form of hierarchy in which the standing of one section of the population is premised on the debasement of others."[126]

Beltrán elaborated further in an NPR interview, telling the network that "whiteness" is not about just skin color but that it's also an "ideology."[127]

In short, she asserts that "the debasement of others" is a "white thing" and if minorities are doing it, it's because they're trying to be white.

Liberals quite simply have a bigoted worldview. It's sick. But it's sadly a major component of the Left's collective wretchedness.

***

A major intersection in the historic Shaw neighborhood of Washington, D.C., was blocked off for weeks during the summer of 2021 as Black Lives Matter protesters danced, cried, and screamed in the streets in protest over a violent incident at Nellie's, a gay bar.

---

[126] Beltrán, Cristina. "To understand Trump's support, we must think in terms of multiracial Whiteness," *Washington Post*, Jan. 15, 2021. https://www.washingtonpost.com/opinions/2021/01/15/understand-trumps-support-we-must-think-terms-multiracial-whiteness/.

[127] Garcia-Navarro, Lulu. "Understanding Multiracial Whiteness And Trump Supporters," NPR, Jan. 24, 2021. https://www.npr.org/2021/01/24/960060957/understanding-multiracial-whiteness-and-trump-supporters.

A video surfaced in mid-June on social media that year showing a security guard attempting to eject a patron who had been fighting with others inside.

The initial clip that was posted on Twitter appeared to show Keisha Young, twenty-two, being pulled down a set of stairs on her back toward the exit by a man in a uniform. At the foot of the steps, another man jumps on top of the guard and starts hitting him. Then there's a pile on with yet more people.[128]

The incident reportedly took place in the early morning hours of Sunday, June 13. A story in the *Washington Post* quoted Young as saying, "Instead of reasoning with me, the security guard just bum-rushed me."[129] As the paper told it, Young "was attacked without warning after she apparently was mistaken for a different woman accused of sneaking in a bottle of liquor from another establishment."

Benjamin Crump, the illiterate Al Sharpton who allegedly has a law degree, tweeted that Young was "savagely dragged...by her HAIR" and declared that she had been "falsely" accused of bringing the liquor bottle into the bar.[130]

The next day, Nellie's issued a statement saying it had ended its relationship with the contracted security vendor, that it was investigating the incident, and that it was indefinitely closing.[131] Nevertheless, loud protests gathered outside and Left-wing groups in the city put out a set of "demands," including that the bar "give reparations to the

---

128 Crump, Benjamin. Twitter, June 14, 2021. https://twitter.com/AttorneyCrump/status/1404637788213968909.

129 Hermann, Peter. "D.C. bar says it fired security contractor after woman said she was dragged down stairs by guard," *Washington Post*, June 14, 2021. https://www.washingtonpost.com/local/nellies-dc-protest-keisha-young/2021/06/14/626d8d56-cd37-11eb-a7f1-52b8870bef7c_story.html.

130 Crump, Benjamin. Twitter, June 14, 2021. https://twitter.com/AttorneyCrump/status/1404637788213968909.

131 Nellie's Sports Bar, Facebook, June 14, 2021. https://www.facebook.com/NelliesDC/photos/a.107275356772/10158773426861773.

black queer and trans community" and that it remain shut down until all demands were met.[132]

They also wanted the owners to subject themselves to a humiliating public "listening session," wherein, no doubt, protesters would take turns screaming at them and demanding that they apologize for being white. (This was once known in China as a "struggle session," when mobs verbally harassed government dissenters, but in present-day America we call it "listening.")

Three days after the brawl, though, a second video surfaced showing what happened in the moments preceding the spectacle of the woman being pulled down the steps.[133]

In that clip, Young is seen at the top of the stairs with about three other men who are fighting, plus two security guards intervening. Young is raining blows on one of the men who is trying to cover his head with his arms. As Young is absolutely wilding out, a guard reaches over the group of men and yanks Young by the shirt, down the steps to remove her from the physical conflict that she was actively participating in. (This is apparently the moment that Young felt "bum-rushed." Why hadn't they just tried "reasoning" with her?!)

At the protests outside of the bar, activists said, "We're not gonna sit here and let black women be disrespected" and chanted, "Protect black women, respect black women."[134] One demonstrator said, "That's why we out here, because America, because of this white ass establishment, don't respect black women and they damn sure don't respect black people."[135]

But there was a niggling detail about the affair that complicated the cut and dry narrative that Young's black body was violated by the

---

132 DC Ward One Mutual Aid, Twitter, June 22, 2021. https://twitter.com/DCW1MutualAid/status/1407381279734173698/photo/2.

133 Quander, Michael. Twitter, June 16, 2021. https://twitter.com/MikeQ_Reports/status/1405128813999185920.

134 Peterson, Beatrice-Elizabeth. Twitter, June 13, 2021. https://twitter.com/MissBeaE/status/1404220906470363137.

135 Eye Seen That Reaction Channel, Twitter, June 14, 2021. https://twitter.com/_EyeSeenThat/status/1404482651386490896.

hands of white supremacy—the man who put his hands on her is also black.

Shouldn't the specifics make a difference if we're going to throw around phrases like "white-ass establishment"?

Again, Nellie's is a gay bar, and it used to be the most popular one in D.C. Over the years that I've lived in the city—I frequented the place—episodes like Young's with the fighting and rowdy behavior had become common. In the most recent times I've been to the bar, at least half of the patrons were black. On some days, it wasn't unusual for most of them to be.

In essence, I mean that Nellie's is not a "white-ass establishment." To the contrary, at the time of this incident, it more often resembled a BET awards show.

It's moronic but this is what our society is being taught by the Left—academia, the national media, the Democratic Party, and all of the entertainment industry. Claim victimhood based on race, gender, or sexual identity, then make ridiculous demands for compensation. The facts don't matter. The story does, even if it's fake or, at best, incomplete. This is the joyless Left.

The aforementioned *New York Times* columnist Charles Blow, who is black, did this exact thing back in 2015 when he made a bunch of noise about his college-age son being held up by police at Yale.[136]

Blow wrote on Twitter at the time that he was "fuming" over a call he received from his son about having been "accosted" and held up at gunpoint because he fit the description of a criminal suspect.

In follow-up tweets related to the incident, Blow said, "This is exactly why I have no patience for people trying to convince me that the fear these young black men feel isn't real." He also tweeted the phrases "I can't breathe," a reference to Eric Garner, a New York man who died in police custody, and "Black lives matter."

---

[136] Scarry, Eddie. "N.Y. Times' Charles Blow said nothing about cop who arrested his son being black," *Washington Examiner*, June 27, 2015. https://www.washingtonexaminer.com/ny-times-charles-blow-said-nothing-about-cop-who-arrested-his-son-being-black.

In a column for his paper, Blow wrote, "I am reminded of what I have always known, but what some would choose to deny: that there is no way to work your way out—earn your way out—of this sort of crisis. In these moments, what you've done matters less than how you look."[137]

Never did Blow mention what should have been a fairly important fact for his readers. Like Blow and his son, the officer in question was also black.

No matter. Blow got what he wanted. He became a prominent player in the race war that, like today, was burning hot. He was booked on national TV to talk about it.

Likewise, Keisha Young from the Nellie's gay bar episode pursued financial gain by way of a lawsuit. No matter what Nellie's did or could have done, it would have never been enough.

Doug Schantz, the bar owner, posted a note on Facebook a month after the incident with an apology.[138] He said Young was treated "inappropriately, unsafely, and disrespectfully." He reiterated that the security contractor had been fired. "We apologize to her for how she was treated," Schantz said.

He further committed to mandating "inclusion training" (reeducation) for all bar staff and said he had named a local Latino transgender person as a new manager and "director of community engagement."[139]

Reading the whole pathetic statement felt like watching poor Schantz enter the den of a rabid lion, hoping a snack he brought would allow him to slip by the beast unmolested. As anyone who has followed the countless, similar conflicts spun up by Black Lives

---

137 Blow, Charles. "Library Visit, Then Held at Gunpoint," *New York Times*, Jan. 26, 2015. https://www.nytimes.com/2015/01/26/opinion/charles-blow-at-yale-the-police-detained-my-son.html.

138 DC Homos, Twitter, July 16, 2021. https://twitter.com/DCHomos/status/1416117510194307077.

139 Nellie's Sports Bar, Facebook, July 16, 2021. https://m.facebook.com/story.php?story_fbid=10158840806556773&id=20669061772.

Matter groups could predict, Schantz would not escape. He would be mauled.

Collective Action for Safe Spaces, a scam organization (sometimes referred to as an "advocacy group") that Schantz reached out to for bar staff sensitivity courses, rejected his overture, stating it didn't believe Schantz's request was made "in good faith," but instead was mere "damage control."[140]

"We stand with survivors & survivor-led movements for accountability," the group said in a statement. "As of July 16, demands issued by DC organizers...have not been met—including an apology to Keisha Young. Nor has Nellie's management engaged the organizations issuing these demands."

Recall that those demands included that the bar "give reparations to the black queer and trans community" and that it remain closed until all demands were met.

It should be noted again that the entire affair traces back to a physical conflict involving not a single white person. The security guard who put his hands on Young, as she was plowing her fists atop another man's head, is also black.

But that's how these liberal shakedowns work. Intimidate and demand. Anything short of complete submission comes with consequences.

Doug Schantz never should have tried engaging the mob.

Weeks passed wherein potential Nellie's customers were warned off entry by protesters, costing the small business potentially tens of thousands of dollars.

The "racial justice" people are nothing if not delusional and the degree to which they are can't be overstated—nor can the national media's role in reinforcing the hysteria.

---

[140] Grablick, Colleen. "'It Reeked Of Performance': Nellie's Steps Towards Inclusivity Fall Short for Activists," DCist.com, July 20, 2021. https://dcist.com/story/21/07/20/nellies-hiring-ruby-corado-gets-push-back-from-activists/.

A month and a half after the Young incident, the *Washington Post* ran a hagiographic story about the enduring protests that took place in front Nellie's, which were finally coming to an end.

"On a busy Friday night," the story began, "people headed to the well-known, often bustling bar on the corner of Ninth and U streets. But for the last time, the party wasn't inside the bar. It was outside."[141]

Included in the online version of the article was a video with interviews of a couple of protesters. One of them named Afeni said that the boycott against Nellie's "is important because they have showed a blatant disrespect for black people, they have showed a blatant disrespect for the demands of the community and they do not hold themselves accountable." By "accountable," she said she meant "paying reparations," "apologizing" and "atoning for your actions."

The video shows others chanting, singing, and line dancing in the street.

Fae, another demonstrator, said, "The greatest form of resistance is black joy because black people are given the least room to be joyful, are given the least things to be joyful." She said the display was "revolutionary," that "this joy that you see here today, like, that is going to be what gets our demands, along with the hard work and blood and sweat and tears that so many black friends have been putting into this effort."

White supremacy: a black woman molested by a black man.

Revolutionary: hijacking a busy highway intersection for twerking.

In any event, those "demands" Fae spoke of had been met weeks ago. At least the ones that were coherent and relevant to the matter at hand. The owner, Doug Schantz, issued a public apology to twenty-two-year-old Keisha Young, who Schantz said was treated "inappropriately, unsafely and disrespectfully." He fired the contractor

---

141 Hilton, Jasmine. "Protests to boycott Nellie's Sports Bar created summer-long 'joy space' for Black LGBTQ community," *Washington Post*, Aug. 31, 2021. https://www.washingtonpost.com/local/nellies-bar-dc-protest-block-party/2021/08/30/d1e56f1c-0678-11ec-a654-900a78538242_story.html.

that had provided security for the bar. He hired a trans person—of color!—as "director of community engagement." And he attempted to hire Collective Action for Safe Spaces, one of those scamming "sensitivity training" firms, but was rebuffed because the organization said that it didn't believe the overture by Schantz was made "in good faith."

There wasn't much left to do, other than "reparations," which is intentionally never specifically defined by the people who claim to deserve them. All the better to say "it's not enough" whenever they're given something.

This was all over a woman who was ejected from a bar by a bouncer. Conveniently, the author of the story in the *Post*—literally an intern named Jasmine Hilton—didn't bother getting into the details of what actually happened that night. Namely, that the bouncer was as black as it gets.

Only in America, with our miserable liberals, can a bunch of delusional "racial justice" freaks see a black man put his hands on a black woman and conclude that it's an episode of white supremacy.

But the *Post* article did quote a demonstrator named Frankie Seabron, who said that the protests created a "space" where "I can be my whole, total self in a world that continues to tell me that being that is not enough." She added, "When I see Keisha, I see me."

I hope not. Otherwise Seabron might need to be dragged out of a bar, too. But this is why the word "delusional" is appropriate.

In the end, Nellie's was ordered to pay a $5,000 fine and relinquish its liquor license for a full week. The *Washington Post* said this was part of a "compromise" with the city in light of an investigation into the Keisha Young incident by the Alcoholic Beverage Control Board.[142]

What exactly, you might ask, was Nellie's compromising for? A belligerent customer had been evicted so that everyone else could

[142] Hilton, Jasmine. "Nellie's Sports Bar agrees to $5,000 fine, 7-day liquor license suspension," *Washington Post*, Oct. 20, 2021. https://www.washingtonpost.com/local/nellies-dc-liquor-license-sports-bar/2021/10/20/863545ba-31f7-11ec-9241-aad8e48f01ff_story.html.

hopefully enjoy the rest of the night. True, a lot of liberals got angry and made an explicitly nonracial incident about race, but why was that Doug Schantz's problem to remedy? He's a bar owner, not a black youth minister.

***

It's a dream of mine that the Left's neurosis on race will one day be treatable with medication. The entire US population would live happier.

But I'm doubtful. Bitchery is their preferred kind of joy. They thrive on telling people what to do, gaslighting everyone with inconsistent, contradictory declarations in the name of "sensitivity" and, most of all, demanding that you "check your privilege."

The *New York Times* in November 2021 ran an op-ed by former Goldman Sachs executive Edith Cooper under the daring headline, "I Was Told I Have Career Advantages 'as a Black Woman.' Here's How I Replied."[143]

As little as you probably care in how she "replied," I have a point to make, so bear with me.

Cooper claimed in the column that a white male in his sixties had recently told her that open positions on prestigious public committees and boards were slim or nonexistent for his demographic. "All they want are women," he said, according to Cooper. "Edith, you must be in great demand—as a Black woman."

She called it a "microaggression" to suggest that her race and gender would be perceived as "relevant credentials" for a board position. After all, she had been a Goldman Sachs executive and had "run multimillion-dollar, client-facing businesses with large teams of people reporting to me."

Black Girl Magic, y'all!

---

143 Cooper, Edith. "I Was Told I Have Career Advantages 'as a Black Woman.' Here's How I Replied," *New York Times*, Nov. 2, 2021. https://www.nytimes.com/2021/11/02/opinion/culture/board-diversity-black-women.html.

Without a flicker of irony, Cooper then claimed she in fact held her current jobs precisely because of her race and gender. "I'm now on the boards of Amazon and PepsiCo, and I've been on the boards of Slack and Etsy," she said. "The executives and boards of these companies prioritized diversity of experience as critical to their organizations' success. My identity as a Black woman is part of that experience."

lol.

And yet, still, Cooper believed there was a problem with the observation by others that at least some opportunities, maybe even most, were extended to her based in large part on her race and that she has a uterus. And she addressed it with the utmost condescension that liberals have developed over years of practice.

She wrote: "'Listen to what you just said,' was my immediate reaction to the person who made the comment about his lost opportunities. You've had it your way for decades. It has taken years to get to the point today where corporate leaders are seriously considering equality of opportunity for people of color…"

It's truly awe-inspiring. The Left has been calling for race quotas for decades. And when they get it, it's a problem. Or more accurately, when they get it *and people notice*, it's a problem.

That's precisely what played out at ESPN from the summer of 2020 to summer 2021.

In early July of 2021, the *New York Times* recapped the racial drama that was unfolding at the Disney-owned sports channel, a fairly trivial matter wherein one woman, reporter and host Rachel Nichols, suspected an on-air opportunity she wanted had gone to someone else on account of her race.[144]

---

[144] Draper, Kevin. "A Disparaging Video Prompts Explosive Fallout Within ESPN," *New York Times*, July 4, 2021. https://www.nytimes.com/2021/07/04/sports/basketball/espn-rachel-nichols-maria-taylor.html.

Back in 2020, Nichols, who is white, had hoped to land a prominent job hosting pre- and post-game coverage of the NBA playoffs. The gig instead went to Maria Taylor, who is black.

"I wish Maria Taylor all the success in the world—she covers football, she covers basketball," Nichols said in what was supposed to be a private conversation with a confidante in July 2020. She was complaining about the executives at ESPN. "If you need to give her more things to do because you are feeling pressure about your crappy longtime record on diversity—which, by the way, I know personally from the female side of it—like, go for it. Just find it somewhere else. You are not going to find it from me or taking my thing away."

The call, though, was mistakenly recorded on a video camera that was in Nichols's hotel room and the recording was uploaded to ESPN's servers. Some staffers got ahold of it and it eventually made its way in front of Taylor.

The *Times* report said that black ESPN employees who heard the recording believed that it "confirmed their suspicions that outwardly supportive white people talk differently behind closed doors."

And here is how the *Times* characterized the offense caused by Nichols's phone call:

> "Within ESPN, particularly among the N.B.A. group that works with both Taylor and Nichols, many employees were outraged upon watching the video. They were especially upset by what they perceived as Nichols's expression of a common criticism used by white workers in many workplaces to disparage nonwhite colleagues—that Taylor was offered the hosting job only because of her race, not because she was the best person for the job."

Wait—when did it become contentious for a person to professionally advance and financially gain on account of her race? That is literally what the entire Black Lives Matter movement is about, with every bit of support from the media.

Taylor's most notable moment at ESPN, to date, is when she delivered a wildly long monologue in 2020 related to the death of George Floyd. At the time, she said "the black experience is not easy" and that "my patience left my body when I watched George Floyd take his last breath, so if that didn't affect you and make you want to reassess the way you're gonna address a question that includes racial injustice in our country after you watched that man die in the middle of the street, something's off." (Isn't ESPN where everyone goes for in-depth commentary about police and race?)

What followed Floyd's death was our supposed racial "reckoning," which has reached its zenith with the Biden administration's endless promotion of racial "equity." At its core, that means considering and elevating people first and foremost based on their race, a concept that has been pushed for more than a generation now at every level of American society. That includes corporate media companies like ESPN that have felt the same pressure as everyone else to make hiring, firing, and promotion decisions with race as a factor second to none.

The logical outcome, no matter what way you cut it, is that some opportunities will be denied to white people (the "privileged") purely because they're white. Plum sports hosting jobs aren't available to everyone who wants one. Someone's going to lose to someone else. We're told by every major cultural institution that race should be a determining factor as to who comes out on top.

After seeing the tape, Taylor apparently stopped speaking with Nichols and held a grudge. Why?

Did Taylor land the job over Nichols because she was the most qualified? Maybe. Was race in any way a part of the decision to give the gig to Taylor? There's a good chance it was, and we're simply told to accept that without saying a word. Nichols eventually lost her job with ESPN.[145]

But don't say that race had anything to do with it!

***

Liberals pretend that there's coherence to it, that if you don't get it, it's because you're not trying hard enough. That's nonsense. There's no way to "get it" because it's not based on anything consistent or explainable. To "get it" is to miss the point. The point is subordination and that's easier for liberals to impose when the rest of us are in a perpetual state of confusion and discomfort by their ever-shifting rules and demands related to race, gender, and sexual "identity."

It's nearly impossible anymore to have a pleasant conversation with liberals without them claiming to have been offended, especially when it comes to race. To wit, the *New York Times* in 2021 started a monthly advice column intending to help readers "resolve personal dilemmas involving race, culture and identity" (boriiinnnngg!).

The November edition of that year featured a submission by a woman racked with anxiety over men who inquire about the ethnicity of her friend, who is of Asian descent. "On several occasions," wrote the poor woman, "I've been at a bar or party with an Asian-American friend and when my friend is getting a drink or off to the bathroom, a man (it's always a man) will ask me, 'Where is she from' or 'What type of Asian is she?'"[146]

You could almost see her sweating, unsure whether to lecture the offending party or start flipping over tables.

---

[145] Hernandez, Joe and Retting, Arielle. "Rachel Nichols' ESPN Show Is Canceled After Her Comments About Maria Taylor," NPR.org, Aug. 26, 2021. https://www.npr.org/2021/08/26/1031235088/rachel-nichols-espn-show-canceled-maria-taylor-nba-jump.

[146] Desmond-Harris, Jenée. "How Should I Respond to Creepy Questions About My Friend's Race?" *New York Times*, Sep. 1, 2021. https://www.nytimes.com/2021/09/01/opinion/race-questions.html.

"I really don't know how to deal with this situation productively as an ally," she continued. (She's not just a friend, she's an "ally.") "I usually don't mention it to my friend both because I feel it's my responsibility to deal with it and because we'll probably never see the offending person again."

Note that "as an ally," this white liberal believes she carries the weight of the world on her shoulders in such high-stakes moments. Inquiries about her friend are her solemn responsibility to address and she desperately needed answers.

"How should I handle these sorts of perpetual-foreigner questions?" she asked. "Should I tell my friend when it happens?"

If you aren't suspended in awe by this scenario all too common for white liberals, the advice offered by columnist Jenée Desmond-Harris really should get you going.

She answered the reader by first explaining that the men asking about her friend are "at least to some extent fetishizing your friend's ethnicity," and are suffering from "yellow fever."

Desmond-Harris advised the woman to "find out how your friend sees these kinds of questions," but cautioned her not to "act as if you're breaking news when you share what's been happening." She further suggested asking the friend if a response to the curious men along the lines of, "My friend doesn't like it when guys fixate on her ethnicity, so I'm not going to talk about it with you" would be sufficient.

None of this is a joke. That submitted question and the accompanying advice actually appeared in the country's most important newspaper. And that helpful tip from Desmond-Harris is precisely why the Left is so antisocial. They don't know how to have normal encounters because everything to them is a fight, a conflict, a confrontation. No matter how trivial the issue.

Here's some real advice for people like this fraught white liberal woman: your friend is probably attractive and that's why men are curious about her. If you're the ugly friend, don't take the overtures from well-meaning strangers as opportunities to quash the potential for love. Nobody likes a cockblock. Instead, consider telling the men that they should ask your friend about her background themselves. Or perhaps simply tell them that she's from whatever American city but that her relatives emigrated from whatever Asian country. When your friend returns, introduce the two of them and let her know that you and the gentleman were just discussing her background. Everyone likes talking about themselves to some degree. This is called socializing.

But explaining that is pointless. They enjoy being angry. They prefer spreading discontent. And they would like it if you did, too.

Their preoccupation with race isn't about righting a historical wrong. It's about feeling superior to everyone they disagree with politically. White liberal Democrats are the most racist, discriminatory people on the planet, even as they're sure to keep a few affirmative action spaces open within their ranks as cover. The purpose of using race as a political tool is to intimidate unassuming voters into joining their cause. Nobody likes being called a racist or a bigot.

They can't persuade, so they bully. Liberals are bullies. And just like bullies, liberals are emotionally stunted, broken, and deeply sad people. They cope by inflicting pain on everyone else.

4

"Insurrection," American White Nationalism, and Other Urban Legends of the Toxic Left

One of my favorite things to do when I'm bored and have some time to kill is pull up whatever the latest study is on *the rise of white supremacy* that invariably has the media spun up into a frothy mess. Those ridiculous studies and papers, published now and again by some liberal advocacy group like the Anti-Defamation League or the FBI, are of course intended to keep minorities (Democratic voters) on edge (motivated) and at the same time, keep as many white Americans as possible in a perpetual state of shame (intimidated).

Why are there so many white people terrorizing this country?!

But the point of looking up the full text of any of these reports is to scan the details and find that they, without exception, show no such widespread rise of white supremacy.

True, in a country of 330 million people, we are bound to have one or two actual, breathing racists of any ethnic background and they might even act up. But what we're most assured is the biggest problem is white supremacists.[147]

> "Top law enforcement officials say the biggest domestic terror threat comes from white supremacists."
>
> —*New York Times*, June 15, 2021[148]

> "Homeland Security Dept. Affirms Threat of White Supremacy After Years of Prodding."
>
> —*New York Times*, October 1, 2019[149]

> "The Grave Threats of White Supremacy and Far-Right Extremism."
>
> —*New York Times*, February 22, 2019[150]

Even under Donald Trump—especially under Donald Trump—the permanent bureaucracy had been hyperventilating about "white supremacy" and the existential threat it supposedly represented to every American, and even democracy itself.

---

147 Kanno-Youngs, Zolan and Fandos. Nicholas. "D.H.S. Downplayed Threats from Russia and White Supremacists, Whistle-Blower Says," *New York Times*, July 1, 2021. https://www.nytimes.com/2020/09/09/us/politics/homeland-security-russia-trump.html.

148 Sullivan, Eileen and Benner, Katie, "Top law enforcement officials say the biggest domestic terror threat comes from white supremacists," *New York Times*, June 15, 2021. https://www.nytimes.com/2021/05/12/us/politics/domestic-terror-white-supremacists.html.

149 Kanno-Youngs, Zolan. "Homeland Security Dept. Affirms Threat of White Supremacy After Years of Prodding," *New York Times,* October 1, 2019. https://www.nytimes.com/2019/10/01/us/politics/white-supremacy-homeland-security.html.

150 T. Cullen, Thomas. "The Grave Threats of White Supremacy and Far-Right Extremism," *New York Times*, February 22, 2019. https://www.nytimes.com/2019/02/22/opinion/christopher-hasson-extremism.html.

Strangely enough, though, there isn't a ton of publicly available government data on the topic. More often than not, a government agency or official makes an assertion about white supremacists on a rampage and we're just supposed to take it as fact without hearing any specifics. For a threat so pervasive, prolific, and prominent, wouldn't you expect there to be a nearly unlimited body of work readily available for the public to consume and understand just how grave it is?

It's not there. You're just supposed to believe it's true.

Sorry, government, but would you mind showing me your work on this thing you're telling me is imminently deadly?

Shut your racist mouth!

In the final months of Trump's term, Acting Homeland Security Secretary Chad Wolf released a report titled "Homeland Threat Assessment."[151] In that report, Wolf said he was "particularly concerned about white supremacist violent extremists who have been exceptionally lethal in their abhorrent, targeted attacks in recent years."

The report said that domestic violent extremists, "specifically white supremacist extremists (WSEs)" were and would continue to be "the most persistent and lethal threat in the Homeland." It made all kinds of claims about "WSEs": that they have "demonstrated longstanding intent to target racial and religious minorities, members of the LGBTQ+ community, politicians, and those they believe promote multiculturalism and globalization"; and "have conducted more lethal attacks in the United States than any other DVE (domestic violent extremist) movement"; and "have engaged in outreach and networking opportunities abroad."

There was even a tally purporting that nearly forty people had been killed in attacks perpetrated by "WSEs" from 2018 and 2019. "WSEs conducted half of all lethal attacks (8 of 16), resulting in the majority of deaths (39 of 48)," the report said.

---

[151] "Homeland Threat Assessment October 2020," Department of Homeland Security, Oct. 6, 2020. https://www.dhs.gov/sites/default/files/publications/2020_10_06_homeland-threat-assessment.pdf.

But there was a problem with the report. There were precisely zero citations showing where the Department of Homeland Security had derived its conclusions—no news articles or academic papers. Just an assurance by the acting secretary, who was "particularly concerned about white supremacist violent extremists" of late.

Hmm...might there be information elsewhere? A document published the previous year by the same department said that the agency looked at the years from 2000 to mid-2016 and counted "28 attacks in the United States committed by WSEs, which collectively resulted in 51 fatalities."[152]

That factoid came with a citation, so that's good. But this was the corresponding footnote: "Based on a review of US Government information, law enforcement reporting, and open source."There was no link to specific incidents or verifiable data. There was no cross reference. In other words, the government just wanted you to trust them on that one!

Is that the best the Feds can do? There's more publicly available information about the government spending millions of dollars to investigate the prevalence of obesity in lesbians than there is about an allegedly serious and fatal threat we're facing from white supremacists.[153]

What about at the state level? In 2019, Democrat New Jersey Governor Philip Murphy's administration published a report on individual episodes of "domestic terrorism" that purportedly took place across the nation throughout the previous year. To the department's credit, it was highly transparent about what it was counting

---

152 "Reference Aid: US Violent White Supremacist Extremists," Department of Homeland Security, September 2017. https://www.dhs.gov/sites/default/files/publications/US%20White%20Supremacist%20Extremists_CVE%20Task%20Force_Final.pdf.

153 Hicks, Josh. "Why the federal government spent $3 million to study lesbian obesity," *Washington Post*, Sep. 4, 2014. https://www.washingtonpost.com/news/federal-eye/wp/2014/09/02/why-the-federal-government-spent-3-million-to-study-lesbian-obesity/.

as an incident of "terrorism," including names, dates, and locations of the perpetrators.

There were, the report said, a total of thirty-two "domestic terrorist attacks, disrupted plots, threats of violence, and weapons stockpiling by individuals with a radical political or social agenda." Of that thirty-two, the office said the overwhelming majority, twenty-five, were carried out by white supremacists.

The report listed each individual incident of white supremacist-linked terrorism, with the name of the perpetrator, his age, and the location of the incident, but without references to where it drew the data. Additional information requires looking up each episode. As it so happens, I did, and anyone else who did the same would see that something wasn't right.

One of the incidents included in the report involved Benjamin Morro, a twenty-eight-year-old Wisconsin man who accidentally killed himself by mishandling explosives in his apartment. No motive has ever been established as to why Morro had the combustible items, but law enforcement claimed to have found "white supremacist material," i.e., literature in pamphlets or books, in his home.[154]

Is a dummy who accidentally blows himself up what comes to mind when you hear the phrase "white supremacist terrorist attack"?

Another one involved Ronnie Wilson, a thirty-two-year-old Tennessee man who was charged with shooting a cop during a traffic stop. Wilson was allegedly a member of the white supremacist gang Aryan Nations, but the officer he shot was also white.

When a white man shoots another white man, is that what comes to mind when you hear the phrase "white supremacist terrorist attack"?

---

[154] Eltagouri, Marwa. "Wisconsin man who blew himself up might have been white supremacist making ISIS-style bombs," *Washington Post*, April 13, 2018. https://www.washingtonpost.com/news/post-nation/wp/2018/04/13/wisconsin-man-who-blew-himself-up-might-have-been-white-supremacist-making-isis-style-bombs/.

One other incident involved a homeless man who was yelling racial epithets in public. (To which I ask, has anyone seen or heard from Chris Matthews lately?)[155]

Yet another pertained to a black man who was burned alive by his white housemate. The two of them lived at Frazier Young Supportive Living, a residence in Tennessee for the mentally impaired.[156]

A homeless man and a literal mental patient. Is that what comes to mind when you hear the phrase "white supremacist terrorist attacks"?

If those four incidents don't fill you with fear that white supremacists lurk in the shadows to commit random acts of violence, I don't know what to tell you. You should be deathly afraid!

To be sure, not all of the entries in the New Jersey government's report are a reach. There are a few that appear to be legitimate, racially motivated attacks on ethnic minorities.

One involved Natasha Bowers, a thirty-three-year-old woman who, along with five other skinheads beat up a black man in the back of a bar in Pennsylvania. But the odd thing about that solitary episode is that it was counted by the report as six separate attacks, one for each of the attackers charged by police.

The authors of the report did the same thing with the assault of a black man at a bar in Washington state.[157] There were eight attackers identified by law enforcement and who were believed to be affiliated with the Aryan Brotherhood. Each suspect was listed in the report as

---

155 Tonsing, Ab. "Man arrested downtown, accused of assault, racial slurs," *The Herald-Times*, June 1, 2018. https://www.heraldtimesonline.com/story/news/local/2018/06/01/man-arrested-downtown-accused-of-assault-racial-slurs/46997893/.

156 Hineman, Brinley. "John Carothers gets life in prison for burning death of housemate at Murfreesboro facility," *Murfreesboro Daily News Journal*, July 22, 2019. https://www.dnj.com/story/news/2019/07/22/tennessee-man-sentenced-murfreesboro-housemates-fiery-death/1777753001/.

157 Johnson, Gene. "Police, FBI probe suspected white supremacist attack on DJ," *Associated Press*, Dec. 10, 2018. https://www.wtae.com/article/police-fbi-probe-suspected-white-supremacist-attack-on-dj/25463630#.

an individual "white supremacist attack," even though there was only one incident.

This would be like saying we had nineteen separate September 11s because that's the number of hijackers who participated. No, we had just the one carried out by multiple people. That more than one attacker was involved doesn't mean we count each one as an individual event.

To recap: of the twenty-five attacks labeled in the New Jersey government's report as white supremacy, fourteen of them were related to only two separate incidents; one of them involved a man who accidentally killed himself; another was perpetrated by a homeless guy; and yet another was committed by a mental patient in a home for the intellectually disabled. That brings the total attacks in 2018 down to more like eight—across our entire nation of 330 million people.

Fewer than ten "white supremacy" attacks doesn't exactly sound like something the FBI should be busying itself with. The numbers on "white supremacy" couldn't have been more padded if they were on their period.

This is an exercise that you can do with every single one of these reports and studies.

In the spring of 2021, the Left-wing Anti-Defamation League (ADL) put out one of its regular reports alleging that overwhelming violence and threats are coming from white supremacists, neo-Nazis, and otherwise Right-wing political groups.

This time, the ADL sounded the alarm with a study claiming that "propaganda" distributed by white supremacists had spiked in 2020. But, as per usual, a look at the details reveals it to be a fraud.[158]

"ADL's Center on Extremism (COE) tracked a near-doubling of white supremacist propaganda efforts in 2020," the report said, "which included the distribution of racist, antisemitic and anti-LGBTQ fliers, stickers, banners and posters."

---

[158] "White Supremacist Propaganda Spikes in 2020," Anti-Defamation League, March 2021. https://www.adl.org/white-supremacist-propaganda-spikes-2020.

Gosh, that sounds awful! Who among us decent Americans would have been passing out such hateful material?

Here's a hint: if you had any material reading the words "America First," it was you. Seriously. That phrase was an example of "white supremacist propaganda," according to the ADL.

Also, if you weren't a fan of the months of rioting perpetrated by the Black Lives Matter activists throughout 2020 and 2021, the ADL might have been referring to you, too. The report stated that a group called "Patriot Front," which the ADL considers to be white supremacist, "continues to avoid using traditional white supremacist language and symbols in its messaging, instead using ambiguous phrases such as 'America First,' 'United we stand,' 'Better Dead Than Red,' 'Two Parties. One Tyranny,' [and] 'Reclaim America.'"

Hilarious. "Better dead than red," a longtime anticommunist catchphrase, had become white supremacy language, according to the ADL.

Another example in the report was the slogan "Open Borders Spread Disease." That's interesting because at the time of the report's publication, it was the heat of a pandemic, and President Biden had considered restricting interstate travel to and from Florida when the state was enduring a surge in cases. No one at the ADL called that closed-border proposal "white supremacy."

To be sure, the report did identify some printed slogans from certain groups that would be considered by normal people to be hateful. But by including "United we stand" as an example of bigotry, I can't help but wonder why the ADL felt the need to pad the numbers.

Well, again, they always do this.

In 2019 the ADL published a report on "Murder and Extremism in the United States in 2018."[159]

---

[159] "Murder and Extremism in the United States in 2018," Anti-Defamation League, January 2019. https://www.adl.org/media/12480/download. That one said that 2018 "was a particularly active year for right-wing extremist murders."

Sounds terrible. But, no. One more time, the specifics didn't really back up the hysteria.

Examples in the study of "right-wing extremist murders" were absolutely absurd. Here's one: "Richard Starry shot and killed four relatives at a local nursing center and at his home in an apparent act of domestic violence before killing himself. According to local media, Starry had been a member of a white supremacist group while in prison."

I don't know about you but when I hear about a white supremacist going on a murderous rampage, I assume there's something relevant to the killings so far as his "white supremacy" goes, and not that the victims involved are his other elderly white family members.

Here's another from that grossly misleading report: "James Mathis, a member of the Georgia-based white supremacist prison gang Ghostface Gangsters, and his wife, Amanda Oakes, allegedly killed their six-month-old son and put his body in a freezer in a hotel room."

Undeniably gruesome? Yes. A sobering reminder that white hoods are burning crosses in front yards across the nation? Not exactly.

The ADL is a racket. And each one of these reports is just as fraudulent as the next. Fear-mongering about an imaginary, racist threat is an ugly thing for the Left to do. Liberals know that and they sleep just fine. Awfulness is their natural state of existence.

***

The riot on Capitol Hill after the 2020 election is one of the most boring, overblown stories of the Trump era, but naturally, Democrats and the media obsess over it because they think it makes Republicans look bad. Oh, and because it gives them an excuse to talk about one of their favorite things—themselves.

It's hard not to gag on the melodrama.

"11 Journalists on Covering the Capitol Siege: 'This Could Get Ugly.'"

—*New York Times*, January 9, 2021[160]

"First Person: A Reporter's Recollections of the Capitol Riot."

—NPR, May 19, 2021[161]

"Journalists describe in vivid detail how January 6 shredded the rule that reporters shouldn't become the story."

—Business Insider, October 28, 2021[162]

"Almost a year after Jan. 6, two journalists release their book 'The Steal.'"

—NPR, January 1, 2022[163]

---

160 Robertson, Katie and Hsu, Tiffany. "11 Journalists on Covering the Capitol Siege: 'This Could Get Ugly,'" *New York Times*, January 9, 2021. https://www.nytimes.com/2021/01/09/business/media/journalists-capitol-mob.html.

161 Bauman, Anna. "First Person: A Reporter's Recollections Of The Capitol Riot," NPR, May 19, 2021. https://www.wbur.org/onpoint/2021/05/19/first-person-a-reporters-recollections-of-the-capitol-riot.

162 Rojas, Warren, Nawaguna, Elvina, and Epstein, Kayla. "Journalists describe in vivid detail how January 6 shredded the rule that reporters shouldn't become the story," *Business Insider*, October 28, 2021. https://www.businessinsider.com/journalists-describe-covering-january-6-capitol-attack-insurrection-2021-10.

163 Gura, David and Hensel, Danny. "Almost a year after Jan. 6, two journalists release their book 'The Steal,'" NPR, January 1, 2022. https://www.npr.org/2022/01/01/1069610988/almost-a-year-after-jan-6-two-journalists-release-their-book-the-steal.

> "One Year Later, Reporters Are Still Processing What Happened on Jan. 6."
>
> —CNN, January 2, 2022[164]

And my personal favorite…

> "'So, So Angry': Reporters Who Survived the Capitol Riot Are Still Struggling."
>
> —Vice, July 6, 2021[165]

There was a total of, perhaps, $1.5 million worth of damage to the Capitol building that day and five people died, all of whom were Trump supporters. Only one individual was killed as a direct result of violence—Ashli Babbitt, an unarmed woman shot by a cop.[166]

By contrast, the endless BLM bonfires of 2020, known by the media as "mostly peaceful protests," resulted in at least $2 billion of property damage[167] and no less than twenty-five riot-related deaths.[168]

But the reporters who happened to be at the Capitol on that day are survivors! The Trump supporters—white people!—were angry! So, so angry!

---

164 Maruf, Ramishah. "One year later, reporters are still processing what happened on Jan. 6," CNN, January 2, 2022. https://www.cnn.com/2022/01/02/media/reliable-sources-jan-6-insurrection-anniversary/index.html.

165 Joseph, Cameron. "'So, So Angry': Reporters Who Survived the Capitol Riot Are Still Struggling."—Vice, July 6, 2021. https://www.vice.com/en/article/4avqqn/reporters-survived-capitol-riot-struggling.

166 "One Year Since the Jan. 6 Attack on the Capitol,"United States Department of Justice. https://www.justice.gov/usao-dc/one-year-jan-6-attack-capitol.

167 Zilber, Ariel. "REVEALED: Widespread vandalism and looting during BLM protests will cost the insurance $2 BILLION after violence erupted in 140 cities in the wake of George Floyd's death," *Daily Mail*, Sep. 16, 2020. https://www.dailymail.co.uk/news/article-8740609/Rioting-140-cities-George-Floyds-death-cost-insurance-industry-2-BILLION.html.

168 Beckett, Lois. "At least 25 Americans were killed during protests and political unrest in 2020," the *Guardian*, Sep. 13, 2020. https://www.theguardian.com/world/2020/oct/31/americans-killed-protests-political-unrest-acled.

Admittedly, there really were some angry Americans on scene that day. They're on video vandalizing public property, entering a government building for the purpose of stalling democratic business, and assaulting police officers. Misconduct did occur.

But the context of what happened leading up to that day and what happened moments ahead of rioters entering the Capitol demonstrates a far different series of events than what the media have portrayed for more than a year.

First, there's the 2020 groundwork, wherein millions of Americans were ordered by federal and state officials to shut down their businesses—their hopes, their dreams, everything they'd worked for their whole lives—and indefinitely lock themselves up at home away from moms, dads, grandmothers, grandfathers, friends, and other loved ones. Compounding the issue, those same officials encouraged and excused mass gatherings and even lawless rioting in the name of "racial justice" following the death of George Floyd. Going to church? Go to jail. Going to a BLM bonfire? Be our guest!

Average Americans were told they couldn't visit restaurants, celebrate birthdays together, or even say goodbye to those they love who lay dying in the hospital. Meanwhile Democrats hosted dinner parties, pampered themselves at hair salons, and gathered en masse for their team players, as when the late Democrat Representative John Lewis was remembered in summer 2020 by a congregation of hundreds of his peers in Washington. (Republicans were also present for the ceremony, but it wasn't the GOP telling everyone else to stay home.)

The madness was topped with a bow when judges in swing states overturned regulations, written into law, governing the election process, always with the pandemic as their catchall excuse for demanding that any and every ballot be counted, regardless of when it was received or "found."

Well, how about that! A stack of two thousand uncounted ballots just turned up in Maricopa County, Arizona, at 11:30 p.m. on Election Day! What luck! Oh, what's this?! Another thirty-five hundred over here in Fulton County, Georgia, behind the printer? Imagine!

The highest court in Pennsylvania unilaterally extended the deadline for which mail-in ballots would be valid, citing—what else?—the pandemic, as a special circumstance.[169]

Even the US Supreme Court, freshly stocked with Trump appointees, sided against the authority of the legislature in North Carolina, ruling that a mail-in-voting deadline extension by the state's Board of Elections would stand because of the pandemic.[170]

As sure as I am that a new disease causing mass death would be reason to encourage mail-in voting, I've never figured out why it would be necessary to change deadlines regarding a date that never changes. It would be like requesting in October that Christmas Day be pushed back a week because, didn't you hear? We're in a pandemic! Yes, and we knew that Christmas Day was coming, as it does every year, at the exact same time, so what's the extra time for?

In any event, the Trump campaign and state-level Republican Party chapters around the country litigated the mess and came up short. But at minimum, there is no denying that the election process, and all of the curious new exceptions to voting laws imposed by the courts, spooked close to half of the country's voters. They made their way to the polls on that first Tuesday of November 2020, cast their ballots, and watched that evening as the election results seemed poised to grant them a victory.

Then they went to sleep, only to wake up and find a different reality the next morning after a shocking number of mail-in ballots were dumped into the tally.

Who wouldn't be confused, suspicious, or highly concerned?

The answer was always the same. *It's a pandemic!*

---

169 Gringlas, Sam. "Pennsylvania Supreme Court Extends Vote By Mail Deadline, Allows Drop Boxes," NPR.org, Sep. 17, 2020. https://www.npr.org/2020/09/17/914160122/pennsylvania-supreme-court-extends-vote-by-mail-deadline-allows-drop-boxes.

170 Durkee, Alison. "Supreme Court Upholds North Carolina's Extended Mail-In Ballot Deadline," *Forbes*, Oct. 28, 2020. https://www.forbes.com/sites/alisondurkee/2020/10/28/supreme-court-upholds-north-carolina-extended-mail-in-ballot-deadline/?sh=6b8d5f57686f.

But wait, you're telling me Joe Biden got eighty-one million votes, more votes than any presidential candidate in US history?

Yes, shut up! It's not hard! This is a pandemic!

Hold on a second. We just endured four years listening to Hillary Clinton squawk that one of the most consequential elections in history was unfair. Not even a month before the 2020 election, she said the 2016 campaign was "not on the level," that, "There's just a lot that I think will be revealed, history will discover," and "you don't win by 3 million votes and have all this other shenanigans and stuff going on and not come away with an idea like, 'Whoa, something's not right here.'"[171] In 2019, she told a sympathetic audience (that for some reason paid to listen to her) that, "You can run the best campaign, you can even become the nominee, and you can have the election stolen from you."[172] At the same time, we sat through a hysterical and seemingly endless investigation into whether Trump was a Russian agent, all at the behest of Democrats and their media allies.

I've got some ques—

> *No you don't! It's a pandemic! The election was free and fair, and you're literally and actively destroying democracy with any suggestion that it wasn't!*

The message was clear: anyone who didn't support the new Democrat regime in Washington wasn't to be heard and, in fact, was likely a fascist white supremacist anyway.

That was the environment in the weeks and months that led to January 6, 2021, when tens of thousands of Americans descended on

---

171 McArdle, Mairead. "Hillary Clinton Maintains 2016 Election 'Was Not on the Level': 'We Still Don't Know What Really Happened,'" *Yahoo News*, Oct. 9, 2020. https://www.yahoo.com/now/hillary-clinton-maintains-2016-election-160716779.html.

172 Cummings, William. "'You can have the election stolen from you,' Hillary Clinton warns 2020 Democrats," *USA Today*, May 6, 2019. https://www.usatoday.com/story/news/politics/onpolitics/2019/05/06/hillary-clinton-warns-2020-democratic-candidates-stolen-election/1116477001/.

Washington for a Stop the Steal Rally intending to send a message that neither the media nor Democrats wanted to hear—the message that their obscene power grab, resulting in billions of dollars of property damage, the literal loss of lives and time with loved ones, all for the sake of winning an election, didn't go unnoticed. And yes, people were angry.

Unfortunately for those people, the new crew in charge would not show them the tolerance and sympathy that they had been showing the Black Lives Matter and Antifa mobs of 2020. Those who showed up in Washington that day would not be viewed as "mostly peaceful" protesters, but "insurrectionists," "white supremacists," "far-right extremists," and "terrorists."

Were there such people at the January 6 protests? Maybe? I would bet you could find a handful, just like you might find a handful of black separationists at a BLM rally. But as the story of that day has come into sharper focus, the truth is far stranger than the enduring narrative built up by the media. The truth is that many of the protesters were unjustifiably beaten by Capitol police, prosecuted for laughably petty crimes and perhaps even lured into a trap by the FBI.

First, it's a fact that at minimum, a sizable portion, but probably the vast majority of the men and women who made the trip to Washington, D.C., on January 6 were not there to engage in misconduct, had no intention of disrupting official government proceedings, and had no idea that being at the scene would implicate them in any criminal activity.

A *New York Times* podcast the week of the first anniversary of the riot—yes, it has an "anniversary" now, because it's a holiday—featured reporter Alan Feuer remarking to host Michael Barbaro about the "whole other group of people that, at least from what we saw that day, seemed to be different." He said that they "appeared to have wandered into the [Capitol] building," where they were "walking around taking pictures of the Capitol. You know, some of them were live-streaming themselves as they posed in front of statues and congress members' offices." In other words, these were the people who were not threatening and, by all indications, not in any way hostile.

Ah, but that distinction doesn't serve the Left's purpose. Feuer went on to say, "Even though it seemed like they weren't doing all that much, they were part of the mob and the fact is, without their collective physical presence, January 6 doesn't happen."

Absurd. This would be like watching someone at a shooting range fire his weapon at another person and concluding that everyone on site bears blame because, after all, they were either holding guns themselves or, by their very presence, permitting some form of violence.

Charges related to January 6 that so many people are facing make it plain that this was not the carnage that the media so desperately wanted the public to believe it was.

Let's just take a few examples, some of which were yet to be adjudicated as of this writing:

- In June 2021, forty-nine-year-old Anna Morgan-Lloyd was sentenced to three years of probation after pleading guilty to one charge of "parading, demonstrating, or picketing in a Capitol Building."[173]
- In October 2021, Robert Reeder, fifty-five, was sentenced to three months of jail time for the same offense.[174]
- Frank Scavo, fifty-eight, was sentenced in November 2021 to two months of incarceration for the same offense. (The two

173 Zantow, Emily. "Indiana grandmother becomes first person sentenced over Capitol riot on Jan. 6," *Washington Times*, June 23, 2021. https://www.washingtontimes.com/news/2021/jun/23/anna-morgan-lloyd-indiana-grandmother-sentenced-ca/.

174 Fischer, Jordan, et al., "'I'm radioactive' | Maryland man sentenced to 3 months in jail says Capitol riot has ruined his life," WUSA9.com, Oct. 8, 2021. https://www.wusa9.com/article/news/national/capitol-riots/im-radioactive-maryland-man-robert-reeder-sentenced-to-3-months-in-jail-says-capitol-riot-has-ruined-his-life/65-8f75b9bc-aed0-4e93-b20a-edbd5893d125.

months was well more than the two weeks that even the prosecutors asked for, the apparent result of a grumpy judge.)[175]

- In December 2021, a sixty-one-year-old by the name of Jennifer Parks was sentenced to two years of probation for the same offense.[176]
- Gary Wickersham, eighty-one, was sentenced the same month to three years of probation for the same offense.[177]
- Twenty-four-year-old Andrew Ericson was sentenced to two years of probation, literally because he entered Nancy Pelosi's office, took a beer out of a refrigerator, and shared some selfies on Snapchat.[178]

These are people who committed the severe crime of having entered a government building to walk around and take photos. (If they had only bothered to schedule a tour, they wouldn't have had federal prosecutors with unlimited resources breathing down their necks about it.) BuzzFeed News fully captured the magnitude of the

---

[175] Hawkins, Samantha. "Capitol rioter's 2-month sentence is harsher than what prosecutors sought," *Courthouse News Service*, Nov. 22, 2021. https://www.courthousenews.com/capitol-rioters-2-month-sentence-is-harsher-than-what-prosecutors-sought/.

[176] Hartle, Sam. "Leavenworth woman sentenced to probation for role in Jan. 6 riot, KSHB41, Dec. 8, 2021. https://www.kshb.com/news/local-news/leavenworth-woman-sentenced-to-probation-for-role-in-jan-6-riot.

[177] Conde, Ximena. "Chesco man, 81, gets home detention and probation after acquaintances reported him to FBI for his involvement in Capitol riot," *Philadelphia Inquirer*, Dec. 21, 2021. https://www.inquirer.com/news/pennsylvania/gary-wickersham-capitol-attack-sentenced-home-detention-20211221.html.

[178] Criminal complaint, U.S. v Andrew C. Ericson, Jan. 20, 2021. https://www.courthousenews.com/wp-content/uploads/2021/12/Ericson-capitol-complaint.pdf.

situation in April 2021 with the headline, "Alleged Jan. 6 Rioters Tried to Steal Signs, Booze, and a Fox News Football from the Capitol."[179]

Sounds truly horrifying.

Even by the Justice Department's own count a year after the riot, out of 725 arrests made, just seventy-five of the defendants were charged with "using a deadly or dangerous weapon or causing serious bodily injury to an officer." Ten individuals were charged with either assaulting a member of the media or destroying their equipment. The rest were charged with trespassing, some form of resisting an officer, or "impeding officers or employees.[180]

This, the public was told by President Biden, is the makeup of the "worst attack on democracy since the Civil War," a multiyear conflict that may have resulted in the death of 750,000 American soldiers.[181]

To be sure, there were some involved that day who received harsher sentences. One man, fifty-four-year-old Robert Palmer, was accused of attacking an officer with a wooden plank and fire extinguisher. He was given a five-year sentence.[182] Jake Angeli, thirty-four, known as the "QAnon Shaman," got about two-and-a-half years of prison time for the charges of trespassing and, again, "Parading, Demonstrating, or Picketing in a Capitol Building."[183]

By the charges alone, it looked less like the Civil War and more like *Night at the Museum.*

---

179 Teruya, Lauren. "Alleged Jan. 6 Rioters Tried to Steal Signs, Booze, and a Fox News Football from the Capitol," *BuzzFeed*, April 9, 2021. https://www.buzzfeednews.com/article/laurenteruya/capitol-riot-building-damage-theft.

180 "One Year Since the Jan. 6 Attack on the Capitol," Department of Justice, Dec. 30, 2021. https://www.justice.gov/usao-dc/one-year-jan-6-attack-capitol.

181 "Who, What, Why: How many soldiers died in the US Civil War?" *BBC*, April 4, 2012. https://www.bbc.com/news/magazine-17604991.

182 Lucas, Ryan. "Capitol rioter who attacked police is sentenced to more than 5 years in prison," NPR.org Dec. 17, 2021. https://www.npr.org/2021/12/17/1065304172/robert-palmer-capitol-riot-jan-6-sentence.

183 "CHANSLEY, Jacob Anthony (aka Jacob Angeli)," Department of Justice, Nov. 22, 2021. https://www.justice.gov/usao-dc/defendants/chansley-jacob-anthony.

It remains in serious dispute as to how it's possible that a crowd of angry voters were able to make their way inside the halls of Congress, in one of the most security-heavy cities in the world, without mass violence. But there is plenty of evidence that, at least at certain entry points, violence wasn't needed. The rioters were simply allowed in and asked by Capitol police to be courteous and respectful.

To wit, a video exists showing precisely that. "The police here are willing to work with us and cooperate peacefully, like our First Amendment allows," one protester says over a megaphone inside the Capitol building. An officer in uniform is then seen telling the protestors, "Do you understand? Show us no attacking, no assault, remain calm." The first man who had the microphone then addresses the rioters, "We're not going to assault, we're going to be heard. Everybody, this must be peaceful." Jake Angeli, the "shaman" adorned in paint and dressed in animal skin, then chimes in as well. "This has to be peaceful. We have the right to peacefully assemble."[184]

Another video shows police officers retreating from entryways, not in a panic, but merely reposting in different locations to further monitor protesters who are seen walking along the halls and gazing at the architecture.[185]

Yet another hilariously shows an officer kindly holding the door for protesters exiting the building, as one says, "We been in there, ain't nothing going on in there." Another one jokes, "It was warm."[186]

None other than CNN reported on a photograph apparently showing a Capitol cop allowing a rioter to capture a selfie with him. Jake Tapper remarked on the "cell phone video" that seemed "to show

---

184 Kelly, Julie. "Video Shows U.S. Capitol Police Gave Protesters OK to Enter," American Greatness, May 16, 2021. https://amgreatness.com/2021/05/16/video-shows-u-s-capitol-police-gave-protesters-ok-to-enter/.

185 "**CAUGHT on CAMERA** Extended Version: Rioters breach the halls of Congress. Shots Fired. 4 Dead," *RMG News*, YouTube, Jan. 7, 2021. https://www.youtube.com/watch?v=V-fkunG5J6k&t=290s

186 Miller, Matthew. Twitter, Jan. 6, 2021. https://twitter.com/mattmiller757/status/1346944869588230144

officers outside, opening gates, allowing even more of the mob to storm in."[187]

A reasonable person watching those videos would certainly have to wonder to himself, "What happened? I thought this was the scene of a bloodthirsty mob trying to overthrow the government. These people just look like tourists without a map..."

True, other footage shows Trump supporters in physical conflict with police in riot gear, an intense confrontation that left one officer dead from a stroke, one protester dead from a heart attack, and another protester dead from being trampled.[188]

But naturally, there's more to the story. Testimony and video evidence suggest that police may have provoked at least some of the conflict by using unwarranted force against protesters who were outside of the Capitol and who were not attempting to breach the premise.

Julie Kelly, who has documented all of this extensively at American Greatness, published a video in May 2021 recorded by activist Kash Kelly. In the footage, Kash remarks on the "flashbangs" that police are firing on the crowd, which, from his angle, is mostly just nonviolent protesters making noise and waving flags.[189]

Thomas Webster, fifty-four, is a two-decade veteran of the New York Police Department and protesting that day. He testified to authorities that one officer dealt him "a big sucker punch" to the face after waving him to come closer.[190]

---

187 "Officer appears to pose for selfie with rioter," CNN.com, Jan. 7, 2021. https://www.cnn.com/videos/politics/2021/01/07/capitol-police-response-pro-trump-riots-lead-vpx.cnn.

188 Healy, Jack. "These Are the 5 People Who Died in the Capitol Riot," *New York Times*, Jan. 11, 2021. https://www.nytimes.com/2021/01/11/us/who-died-in-capitol-building-attack.html.

189 Kelly, Julie. "New Video Depicts Capitol Police Using Stun Grenades on Crowd," *American Greatness*, May 27, 2021. https://amgreatness.com/2021/05/27/new-video-depicts-capitol-police-using-stun-grenades-on-crowd/.

190 Kelly, Julie. "Did Cops Attack and Provoke Peaceful Protesters on January 6?" American *Greatness*, June 28, 2021. https://amgreatness.com/2021/06/28/did-cops-attack-and-provoke-peaceful-protesters-on-january-6/.

Yet another video shows how police, under no apparent threat—no one is pushing, no one is advancing on the Capitol—began tossing smoke grenades into the crowd of protesters outside of the building. Women can be heard screaming. One man says, "Wow, that fucking hurt." Another says, "That got me."[191]

Protestors responded to the aggression with the chant, "Decertify! Decertify!" a reference to the electoral vote certification that was being led that day by Vice President Mike Pence. At one point, they sang "The Star-Spangled Banner."

One woman, Victoria White, said in a recorded video that she had been taken into custody by police after she was pepper sprayed and beaten over the head by an officer with a baton. White was among the throngs of Trump supporters and police crammed into the Capitol's west terrace tunnel, as famously seen in graphic images. She said she had thought entering the channel would lead to another entrance to the building, but that when she got inside, she faced a wall of police with massive shields and became stuck between them and the crush of people following her.

"[W]hen they are pushing, you have to understand, it's like a mass of people," White said. "A lot of people crammed together and, ya know, the police are right there and they were like, spraying everyone, like macing them. And then I look at a police officer and I'm like, 'You took an oath to the Constitution,' and apparently that didn't sit so well with him, and he decided to hit me really hard on the head with a metal baton. And then the next thing I know there's more hits coming, more mace coming at us, everyone there…"[192]

An FBI complaint against White described the incident. "As the video progresses, the MPD officers attempt to push WHITE back with their riot shields and fend her off with a baton," the document

---

191 Hudson, Glenn. "Stop the steal protest Washington D.C Jan. 6th 2021," YouTube, Jan. 8, 2021. https://www.youtube.com/watch?v=MrW1bD9laoU.

192 Affidavit, Department of Justice, April 7, 2021. https://www.justice.gov/usao-dc/case-multi-defendant/file/1385541/download.

said. "WHITE is seen in a red sweater, and it appears that she is attempting to grab a shield and uses her hand to block the baton."

A photo in that same document shows White in police custody, her face streaked with blood. Security camera footage from the clash in the tunnel does appear to show her trying to heave herself up over the crowd, perhaps to relieve herself from the crush, only to be repeatedly bludgeoned by the baton and also punched by an officer.[193]

In an interview with Julie Kelly, White also claimed that she felt the hand of another officer grab her by the hair and shake her head back and forth.[194]

Other Trump supporters who made their way or found themselves in the same tunnel also have testified that they witnessed police physically assaulting unarmed women. Ryan Nichols, a retired US Marine who was charged in relation to the riot, told Kelly, "When I saw women being beaten and in distress, my rescue instinct kicked in and I knew I had no choice but to help rescue them."[195]

You could doubt the accounts of any one of these people. They are, after all, charged with criminal conduct. But the videos certainly don't lie. And to the extent that law enforcement had anything to do with how bad things turned out, the *New York Times* reported in September 2021 that the FBI had in fact infiltrated the Proud Boys, a Right-wing men's group that was in attendance at the protest.[196]

According to the *Times*, the FBI was using at least two unnamed "informants" within the Proud Boys to relay information back to

---

193 McBride, Joseph. Twitter, Dec. 22, 2021. https://twitter.com/McBrideLawNYC/status/1473837258423902209.

194 Kelly, Julie. "January 6 Police Beating Victim Speaks: 'I Could Have Died,'" American Greatness, Dec. 8, 2021. https://amgreatness.com/2021/12/08/150045/.

195 Kelly, Julie. "Terror in the Capitol Tunnel," *American Greatness*, Nov. 18, 2021. https://amgreatness.com/2021/11/18/terror-in-the-capitol-tunnel/.

196 Feuer, Alan and Goldman, Adam. "Among Those Who Marched Into the Capitol on Jan. 6: An F.B.I. Informant," *New York Times*, Oct. 28, 2021. https://www.nytimes.com/2021/09/25/us/politics/capitol-riot-fbi-informant.html.

law enforcement on the activities taking place in Washington on January 6.

From that article: "As scores of Proud Boys made their way, chanting and shouting, toward the Capitol on Jan. 6, one member of the far-right group was busy texting a real-time account of the march. The recipient was his F.B.I. handler."

And: "The F.B.I. also had an additional informant with ties to another Proud Boys chapter that took part in the sacking of the Capitol, according to a person familiar with the matter..."

Most puzzling is an admission by the newspaper's reporter that the records he analyzed "do not directly address...why he [one of the informants] was cooperating" with the FBI.

So, we don't get to know who the informants are, nor why they were working with the FBI? If they were working with the FBI and presumably able to feed them direct information about what was happening on the ground, why was the preparation and response by law enforcement so shockingly poor?

The *Times* does a nice job attempting to clean up for the FBI on that last question. "[T]he informant's F.B.I. handler was slow to grasp the gravity of what was happening that day," the report said. Oh, so an agent tasked with keeping the Capitol safe was simply "slow"? Okay, then! No biggie!

Does he still have a job? Almost certainly.

There's also the enduring mystery of Ray Epps, the sixty-year-old Arizona man who was captured on video on both January 6 and the day before, urging Trump supporters to breach the Capitol. "I'm going to put it out there," Ray told a crowd of protesters the night before the riot. "I'm probably going to go to jail for it, okay? Tomorrow we need to go into the Capitol. Into the capitol."[197]

The declaration was greeted with a decided lack of enthusiasm. "What? No!" a man is heard yelling back. The crowd then broke into

---

[197] Cruz, Ted. Twitter, Jan. 11, 2022. https://twitter.com/SenTedCruz/status/1481021072367624196 .

chants of, "Fed! Fed! Fed!" suggesting that Epps was probably a federal agent goading them into wrongdoing, which some might refer to as "entrapment."

Shortly before protesters made their way to the Capitol from Trump's speech near the White House, Epps was also seen on the National Mall, imploring anyone who would listen to head toward the Capitol because, "That's where our problems are."[198]

What we know further about Epps is that the FBI initially published and distributed the photographs of several wanted suspects, including Epps, for their alleged participation in the Capitol riot, only to remove his image a day later and without explanation.[199] As of this writing, the FBI has never explained why Epps was dropped from legal pursuit. The silly Democrat-run House "Select Committee" tasked with investigating January 6 did release a statement in January 2022 claiming that Epps had been interviewed by the members and that he denied working for or with the FBI.

Politico lent backup to the Committee, declaring that it had officially "debunked a conspiracy theory" about Epps, and further asserted that Epps "was no secret government agent."[200]

I guess the show's over, *folks*™!

The basis for Politico making those statements was that "there's no indication Epps went into the Capitol on January 6, a factor that prosecutors have weighed heavily when deciding who to charge," and there were "multiple reasons why a potential suspect would be

---

198 Gaetz, Matt. Twitter, Jan. 11, 2022. https://twitter.com/RepMattGaetz/status/1481048203814387714.

199 "Meet Ray Epps: The Fed-Protected Provocateur Who Appears To Have Led The Very First 1/6 Attack On The U.S. Capitol," *Revolver News*, Oct. 25, 2021. https://www.revolver.news/2021/10/meet-ray-epps-the-fed-protected-provocateur-who-appears-to-have-led-the-very-first-1-6-attack-on-the-u-s-capitol/.

200 Cheney, Kyle. "The Jan. 6 panel has debunked a conspiracy theory that popped up even in Congress this week. Ray Epps was no secret government agent," *Politico*, Jan. 11, 2022. https://www.politico.com/minutes/congress/01-11-2022/1-6-conspiracy-disproved/.

removed from the list." In other words, *Politico* was taking the word of a partisan political committee as fact and simply guessing that the FBI—an agency that has been caught lying multiple times in recent years—was being honest.

That's our media today, eagerly swallowing the government line, so long as it's Democrats feeding it to them.

The FBI has further declined to state under oath in Congress whether any FBI informants or agents were involved with the January 6 riot. The secrecy is appalling.

There appears to have been, at minimum, a complete breakdown of law enforcement and intelligence gathering that day. That's something that the media tepidly acknowledged in the immediate months following January 6, before they settled on the preferred narrative that the police were actually all heroes and that the protesters were terrorists and nearly unstoppable.

Here's how the Associated Press reported things just days after the riot: "As the rioters stormed the US Capitol, many of the police officers had to decide on their own how to fight them off. There was no direction. No plan. And no top leadership."[201]

And here was the *New York Times* a few months thereafter: "The Capitol Police had clearer advance warnings about the Jan. 6 attack than were previously known, including the potential for violence in which 'Congress itself is the target.' But officers were instructed by their leaders not to use their most aggressive tactics to hold off the mob..."[202]

It should have been an embarrassment to Capitol Police and a realization in Washington that the half of the country that they had

---

201 Merchant, Nomaan and Long, Colleen. "Police command structure crumbled fast during Capitol riot," *Associated Press*, Jan. 18, 2021. https://apnews.com/article/police-command-structure-us-capitol-riot-a27921d08ca949c0b1e64c33628dd80e.

202 Broadwater, Luke. "Capitol Police Told to Hold Back on Riot Response on Jan. 6, Report Finds," *New York Times*, April 13, 2021. https://www.nytimes.com/2021/04/13/us/politics/capitol-police-riot-report.html.

been fucking with all year by instigating violent race riots and using a deadly pandemic for political gain had finally reached its breaking point. But that's not what happened.

Instead, Democrats and the media heralded the police as valiant, selfless legends, and labeled the protesters "terrorists," "insurrectionists," and, of course, "racists." Joe Biden's attorney general, Merrick Garland, marked the "anniversary" of the riot with a public address promising that more prosecutions would come and with more severe sentencing recommendations by the Justice Department.

"It is impossible to overstate the heroism of the Capitol Police officers, Washington, D.C. Metropolitan Police Department officers, and other law enforcement officers who defended and secured the Capitol that day," Garland said of the police, who everyone knows absolutely shit the bed on January 6.[203]

Responding to pressure from congressional Democrats who felt that the Biden administration had not been vindictive enough, Garland pledged there would be more intense legal action to come. "A necessary consequence of the prosecutorial approach of charging less serious offenses first is that courts impose shorter sentences before they impose longer ones," he assured his masters. "In recent weeks, however, as judges have sentenced the first defendants convicted of assaults and related violent conduct against officers, we have seen significant sentences that reflect the seriousness of those offenses—both in terms of the injuries they caused and the serious risk they posed to our democratic institutions."

The message was clear. Revenge was on the agenda and Biden's DOJ would not let it slip away.

In Biden's own address that day, he swore that "this isn't about being bogged down in the past," while delivering thirty minutes of remarks about an event from a year ago, calling the last president a

[203] Garland, Merrick. Remarks at the Department of Justice, Jan. 5, 2022. https://www.justice.gov/opa/speech/attorney-general-merrick-b-garland-delivers-remarks-first-anniversary-attack-capitol.

loser and accusing the January 6 protesters of representing "the cause to destroy America, to rip us apart."[204]

That's the president who launched his 2020 campaign promising to "restore the soul of America." Restoring our soul apparently involves hyper obsessing over a single half-day of very limited civil unrest that should have caught no one by surprise. It apparently involves repeated reminders of how bitter and savage the 2020 election was and that it was Biden who ended up in the White House.

Let the healing begin!

But this is what truly brings these people their version of joy: punishment and coercion. Try thinking back to a time that Trump or any Republican held on to a political grudge after an election. There isn't one. The Obama years had the "Fast and Furious" international gun-trafficking scandal, the Benghazi scandal, and the IRS-targeting-conservative-nonprofits scandal, to name a few. Regardless of whether you think it's a good thing, none of them were pursued once Obama was out of office and Clinton had failed to win in 2016.

But we're supposed to live with this, a never-ending ghost chase led by Democrats out of pure spite. And Right-wingers are always expected to turn the other cheek and make do while liberals serve out their cocktails of toxic waste.

January 6 should have been a wake-up call that both sides have a breaking point. But it doesn't look like the Left got that message. There will certainly be consequences.

---

[204] Biden, Joe. Remarks at the White House, Jan. 6, 2022. https://www.whitehouse.gov/briefing-room/speeches-remarks/2022/01/06/remarks-by-president-biden-to-mark-one-year-since-the-january-6th-deadly-assault-on-the-u-s-capitol/.

5

Thou Shalt Not Speak Unless Truly Boring

This has been true for a while now, but it keeps getting truer that liberals have entirely lost their capacity to entertain. Contrary to the word "liberal" meaning free, the modern Left is now rigid, intolerant, stubborn, shortsighted, and, worst of all, humorless.

It no longer carries the ability to make people laugh—I mean really laugh, not Stephen Colbert audience "laugh"—or provoke them to think about new ideas from different perspectives.

Ironically, there was a time not long ago when the Left had something Right-wingers deeply envied. That thing was Jon Stewart, a committed Democrat who was both devilishly clever and legitimately funny. Most importantly, he had the coveted opportunity to display those qualities four nights every week on national television.

Stewart was a political factor with more influence than any other liberal Democrat during both the Bush and Obama presidencies. Conservatives would be reluctant to admit it, but they would have killed to have their own Stewart, a happy warrior with a razor wit that routinely devastated Republicans in both his incisive interviews and his compelling monologues that exposed the intellectual weaknesses (and even dishonesties) of the Right.

Conservatives would, again, be loath to concede it, but it's true—Stewart frequently beat them, but ultimately, he made them better. He forced them to smarten up.

But that was a different time. That was when liberals had a sense of humor and the ability to feel genuine joy. They don't have that anymore. Now they have Trevor Noah, a self-serious foreigner who took over for Stewart at Comedy Central's *The Daily Show* in 2015. Unlike Stewart, Noah isn't a charming and shrewd political satirist. There is actually very little indication that he even possesses an original or personal worldview that shapes his presentation. No, Noah is more like a lazy keyboard warrior who gets his "ideas" by scrolling through Twitter to see why other liberals are mad. He seems to spend no time considering whether what he's going to say each night will be new, interesting, or funny at all, but only whether Democrats will signal their agreement with him by sharing clips from his show on Facebook.

In February 2022, when Leftists were still, after more than a month, whining that Joe Rogan had hosted a COVID vaccine skeptic on his podcast show, Noah used one of his monologues to comment on something liberals were already on top of—Rogan's past usage of the n-word—the context of which was in discussing the taboo nature of the word, but liberals were angry anyway.)

Rogan, a TV personality and stand-up comedian, had said in previous episodes of his show that the exclusivity of the n-word felt strange and he used the word multiple times. After those remarks resurfaced, he apologized, explaining that the offending segments were meant to be funny. "We've all swung and missed when it comes to comedy," he said.[205]

---

[205] Nola, Emma. "Joe Rogan Defends 'Missteps' Says Listeners Know He Is 'Trying to Be Funny,'" *The Week*, Feb. 9, 2022. https://www.newsweek.com/joe-rogan-defends-missteps-trying-funny-akaash-singh-podcast-1773-1677475.

A fresh take on the controversy might be that some people also feel that the stigma against incest is strange, but that nonetheless, it is widely accepted as wrong to consider engaging it. Or another view might be that Rogan is right, it is strange, because placing rules on street slang kind of defeats the purpose of casual, irreverent speech.

Of course, Noah didn't pursue anything original. He chose to regurgitate what liberals were already saying on social media—that Rogan is a racist. "And it's not just racist," he said. "Like, let's be honest about it. That's not just racist. That's like O.G. racism. That's like the original, old-school—like, that's from the Mt. Rushmore of racism."[206]

There was no punchline. There was no devastating polemical observation. There was only a virtue signal from Noah to his audience and the larger media, that he understood Rogan was a high-profile enemy of their cause and, therefore, predictably, must be a racist.

The contrast with Noah's predecessor couldn't be starker if it was bleached white. In the summer of 2014, during the heat of the rioting and media outrage over the police shooting death of eighteen-year-old Michael Brown, a black man, Jon Stewart gleefully shivved the dim conservatives in the media who spouted off without being fully informed of what exactly had happened.

Following a slew of clips of Fox News personalities griping that Democratic leaders and the media at large weren't paying the same amount of attention to astronomical levels of crime in places like Chicago, where the vast majority of violence is committed by blacks against other blacks, Stewart showed video of then-President Obama and Al Sharpton addressing that very issue.

"They are trying, actually, to do something," Stewart said of the efforts on black-on-black crime. "You see, you being ignorant of those attempts doesn't mean the issue itself is being ignored, the same way

---

[206] Noah, Trevor. Comedy Central's "The Daily Show," Feb. 8, 2022. https://www.cc.com/episodes/287br5/the-daily-show-with-trevor-noah-february-8-2022-robert-glasper-season-27-ep-55.

that when it snows where you live doesn't mean the world isn't getting hotter."[207]

After showing another clip of yet one more Fox guest saying, "You know who talks about racism? Racists," Stewart asked with a grin, "Did you just 'He who smelt it, dealt it' racism?!"

Even if you disagreed with Stewart, those were legitimately funny and provocative lines.

R.I.P.

Leftist comedians like Noah are simply not funny because the Left has no interest anymore in making people laugh, even when they pretend they do. Name a truly funny and prominent comedian presently heralded by Democrats. I'll wait.

Other than Stewart, it used to be Bill Maher. But because he, like every sane American, has taken notice of the extreme intolerance and mean totalitarian impulses of the new Left, they're not so keen on Maher anymore.

In January 2022, Maher hosted liberal journalist Bari Weiss and the two of them commiserated about their peers who refused to let up on the COVID panic, despite the free and widely available vaccines, plus the indisputable data that lockdowns and restrictions were doing more harm to the public than the virus itself. "I'm done with COVID…It's ridiculous at this point," Weiss said to applause.

For that, *Los Angeles Times* columnist Michael Hiltzik wrote that Maher, "Owes the entire country an apology."[208]

New York Times liberal Michelle Goldberg likewise reacted to Maher's show, insufferably scolding everyone with a lecture that "not everyone has the luxury of being insouciant about infection."[209]

---

207 Stewart, Jon. Comedy Central's "The Daily Show," Aug. 28, 2014. https://www.youtube.com/watch?v=T_98ojjIZDI.

208 Hiltzik, Michael. "We're not really 'done with COVID,'" *Los Angeles Times*, Feb. 8, 2022. https://www.latimes.com/business/story/2022-02-08/is-covid-over-yet.

209 Goldberg, Michelle. "What Does It Mean to Be 'Done With Covid'?" *New York Times*, Jan. 24, 2022. https://www.nytimes.com/2022/01/24/opinion/done-with-covid.html.

Maher was well aware of how deranged his own side has become and their attempts to purge their ranks from anyone who wasn't him or herself bogged down in gloom and bitterness. "I am still the same unmarried, childless, pot-smoking libertine I always was," he said in an episode later that month. "I have many flaws, but you can't accuse me of maturing. Let's get this straight. It's not me who's changed. It's the Left, who is now made up of a small contingent who've gone mental and a large contingent who refuse to call them out for it. But I will. That's why I'm a hero at Fox [News] these days."[210]

He continued, "Which shows just how much liberals have their head up their ass, because if they really thought about it, they would have made me a hero on their media, but that can't happen in this ridiculous new era of mind-numbing partisanship, where if I keep it real about the nonsense in the Democratic Party, it makes me an instant hero to Republicans." He said that he's sometimes confronted by his peers who say, "You know, you didn't used to make fun of the Left as much." His reply to them, he said, is, "Yeah, because they didn't [used to] give me so much to work with."

And as far as liberals losing any sense of humor they once had, Maher said, "The oath of office I took was to comedy. And if you do goofy shit, wherever you are on the spectrum, I'm going to make fun of you because that's where the gold is. And the fact that they (conservatives) are laughing at it should tell you something—it rings true."

It doesn't simply "ring" true. It is manifestly true. Liberals don't bother coming up with anything funny anymore. They now spend their time "canceling" anything funny.

You saw what happened to Dave Chappelle for making a few jokes about transgenderism in his Netflix specials. The jokes were harmless by any measure, and, as with all effective humor, they told a truth. "I am not saying that...transgender women aren't women,"

---

[210] Maher, Bill. HBO's "Real Time," Jan. 28, 2022. https://www.hbo.com/real-time-with-bill-maher/season-20/1-january-28-2022-ira-glasser-fiona-hill-matt-welch.

he said in arguably his most controversial bit on the topic. "I am just saying that those pussies that they got—you know what I mean? I'm not saying it's not pussy but…it tastes like pussy but that's not quite what it is, is it? That's not blood, that's beet juice."

He had used the word "tranny" and told jokes about biological men dominating women's sports leagues. In one segment, he mocked individuals who want their pronouns to be "they" and "them," imagining a scenario in which he's being chased by such a person, but unsure if he should be afraid that it's more than one.

It must have been particularly offensive when Chappelle dared to say out loud that there was a fundamental difference between the two distinct genders, because, "Every human being in this room, every human being on earth, had to pass through the legs of a woman to be on earth."[211]

If this were the worst kind of ridicule transgender people would have to endure, their lives would be, all in all, pretty good. But, again, liberals don't know how to handle jokes. They're no longer quick enough. They've lost their wit.

Leftists at Netflix openly whined about Chappelle's comedy, declaring that it "directly harms trans people."

"I didn't expect my job to include supporting the platforming of hate speech when I woke up today," one employee tweeted, "yet here we are."[212]

There were protests and organized walkouts. Liberal commentators in the media were beside themselves.

Roxane Gay, a social critic who, without shame, writes about the struggles she faces as an obscenely fat person, unironically wrote in the *New York Times* that Chappelle's latest special in late 2021 was, "a

---

211 Chappelle, Dave. "The Closer," Netflix, Oct. 5, 2021.

212 Clark, Travis. "Netflix employees speak out against Dave Chappelle's new special in which he makes transphobic comments," Insider.com, Oct. 7, 2021. https://www.businessinsider.com/netflix-employees-speak-out-against-transphobic-chappelle-comments-2021-10.

joyless tirade of incoherent and seething rage, misogyny, homophobia and transphobia."[213]

Black gay columnist Brian Broome of the *Washington Post* called Chappelle's special "mean."[214]

CNN's website reacted by publishing one of those self-serious pieces about the "disproportionate violence" that transgender people endure[215] (almost all of which involves transgender prostitutes killed by black drug dealers and/or closeted black men.)[216]

To entertain an idea or have a sense of humor about anything requires a relaxed and unthreatened mind. Democrats and the hellions they're raising in academia don't have that. They have strict conformity and demand that everyone else do the same. That's why "canceling" is such a big thing for them, with college campuses serving as ground zero.

The antisocial behavior demonstrated by liberal Democrats in everyday encounters is experienced just the same in academia but on steroids. Universities are supposed to be places for a free exchange of ideas. Now they're where ideas go to die.

Liberals make up the vast majority of school administrations and social sciences and humanities departments. They resent anyone to the right of Ruth Bader Ginsburg and reward their students for showing equal amounts of hostility toward nonconformists.

---

213 Gay, Roxane. "Dave Chappelle's Brittle Ego," *New York Times*, Oct. 13, 2021. https://www.nytimes.com/2021/10/13/opinion/dave-chappelle-netflix-trans.html.

214 Broome, Brian. "Dave Chappelle cannot erase me," *Washington Post*, Oct. 7, 2021. https://www.washingtonpost.com/opinions/2021/10/07/dave-chappelle-the-closer-gay-trans-community/.

215 Cane, Clay. "Dave Chappelle's Trumpian claims of 'cancel culture' are laughable," CNN.com, Oct. 11, 2021. https://www.cnn.com/2021/10/11/opinions/dave-chappelle-netflix-the-closer-cane/index.html.

216 Scarry, Eddie. "The uncomfortable truth about 'Black Trans Lives Matter,'" *Washington Examiner*, June 11, 2020. https://www.washingtonexaminer.com/opinion/the-uncomfortable-truth-about-black-trans-lives-matter.

Dr. Eric Kaufmann, a political science professor at the University of London, investigated patterns of political opinion and discrimination at universities in London, the US, and Canada. In 2021, he released his exhaustive study drawing on surveys and publicly available databases. He found that liberals in academia, both the students and the faculty, tend to create environments perceived as intolerant and unwelcoming of opposing viewpoints. Kaufmann did note that it's a "small minority" but that nonetheless, it is Leftists on campuses who foster an oppressive atmosphere and lead the outsize majority of "cancellations" of student organizations, guest speakers, and academics who might confront them with differing opinions.

Included in Kaufmann's study was research by the Foundation for Individual Rights in Education (FIRE), a speech freedom advocacy group, which showed that between 1998 and 2019, attempts by campus activists to block guest speakers from appearing at the school had steadily inclined. All combined, FIRE tallied 498 campus incidents, only 141 of which were initiated by Right-leaning activists. The Left was responsible for 304 of them, more than doubling the Right. (The rest were attributed to activists on neither the Left nor the Right.)[217]

That liberal student activists are behaving this way is certainly correlated to the overwhelming political makeup of their professors on campus. Kaufmann noted a separate study from 2007 demonstrating that college-level educators were, by far, more likely to be Democrats than Republicans, by an almost four-to-one ratio. In the social sciences and humanities departments (liberal arts subjects like history, journalism, political science, and so forth), it was eight-to-one.[218]

217 FIRE's "Disinvitation Database," Feb. 22, 2022. https://www.thefire.org/research/disinvitation-database/#home/?view_2_sort=field_13|asc&view_2_per_page=500&view_2_page=1.

218 Gross, Neil and Simmons, Solon. "The Social and Political Views of American Professors," Working Paper, September 24, 2007. https://www.researchgate.net/publication/228380360_The_Social_and_Political_Views_of_American_Professors.

A more recent study from 2018 by Mitchell Langbert, a business professor at Brooklyn College of CUNY, puts the ratio of Democrats to Republicans teaching at the university level closer to thirteen-to-one.[219]

In other words, college professors who vote Republican are fairly rare and, by all indications, getting rarer.

Obviously certain industries and careers might be more prone to attract a certain demographic for various reasons. Women make up about three-fourths of public-school teaching positions[220] but only about a quarter of science and engineering jobs.[221] This isn't to suggest that universities should adopt affirmative action for Republicans and conservatives. The problem isn't necessarily that there aren't enough of them, but that they're made by their ideologically opposite peers to feel intimidated and unwanted, something that shouldn't be happening if there is even just one Right-winger on staff.

And that is in fact what happens.

The ideological skew, Kaufmann wrote, "translates fairly readily into a hostile climate for conservative scholars." Conducting his own survey, Kaufmann asked college professors to answer whether "there is a supportive or hostile climate towards people with your political beliefs in your department." Among professors who identified as politically "fairly right," 69 percent said they felt the climate was hostile. Among the "very right," it was slightly higher at 71 percent. By contrast, only 3 percent of those identifying as "fairly left," and 5 percent of the "very left" said they felt the climate was hostile.

---

219 Langbert, Mitchell. "Homogenous: The Political Affiliations of Elite Liberal Arts College Faculty," National Association of Scholars, April 19, 2018. https://www.nas.org/academic-questions/31/2/homogenous_the_political_affiliations_of_elite_liberal_arts_college_faculty.

220 "Characteristics of Public School Teachers," National Center for Education Statistics, May 2021. https://nces.ed.gov/programs/coe/indicator/clr.

221 "Women, Minorities, and Persons with Disabilities in Science and Engineering," National Science Foundation, January 2017. https://www.nsf.gov/statistics/2017/nsf17310/digest/occupation/overall.cfm.

In short, liberals in academia feel very well supported by their peers to be themselves, whereas Right-leaning professors don't get the sense of being nearly so welcome.

It's not like the Democrats on staff don't know what's happening. Kaufmann also asked professors in his survey if they would be comfortable expressing support for either Joe Biden or Donald Trump to a colleague ahead of the 2020 election, depending on whom they supported in the previous presidential race.

Among professors who voted for Trump in 2016, only 3 percent said they would be comfortable stating that they would again vote for him to have a second term. But 97 percent said if they planned on supporting Biden, they would have no problem telling a colleague about it.

The results were pretty much mirrored among professors who voted for Hillary Clinton in 2016. The overwhelming majority, 91 percent, said they would be comfortable telling a colleague that they planned on supporting Biden. Less than 15 percent said they would be comfortable if they were backing Trump. (That the total equaled more than 100 percent likely reflects the small number of Clinton supporters who said they would be comfortable voicing either opinion.)

The self-censorship by Right-wingers that Kaufmann found is truly wild. When it comes to teaching and research, which they're literally paid to do, 70 percent of Republican and conservative professors said they refrain from airing their personal views. Among both "fairly left" and "very left" professors, only 26 percent said the same. Of course. Liberals always feel at liberty to state exactly how they feel, while Right-wingers are preoccupied with dread that they might offend someone.

Even a mild social interaction such as sitting at lunch next to a person with opposing political views is too much for liberal professors. Among Trump-supporting professors surveyed by Kaufmann, more than half, 61 percent, said they would be comfortable dining with a peer who supported the Far-Left Bernie Sanders. Among Clinton-supporting professors, less than half, 41 percent, said they would be comfortable sitting next to a Trump supporter. (Kaufmann did not include information on asking Trump-supporting professors about sitting next to Clinton backers, perhaps because they had heard what happened to Jeffrey Epstein.)

The ultimate effect, naturally, is that competing ideas and arguments are unheard by both professors and students. It creates yet another echo chamber that further narrows the frame of reference through which young people come to view the world. As Kaufmann puts it, "The combination of individual level discrimination by both sides with a heavy Left-leaning majority produces a high degree of system-level bias against conservatives. These findings mean that conservative scholars who self-censor are not paranoid, but acting rationally."

In essence, Right-wing college professors are keeping their opinions to themselves out of self-preservation, in fear that opportunities, resources, or even their jobs could be put in jeopardy should they be more open about them.

"A sufficiently large proportion of academics are willing to penalize work that is right-leaning to make it prudent for conservatives to hide their views," wrote Kaufmann. "This substantiates with data the repeated testimony that there is a climate of political discrimination inside the contemporary university. If conservative academics wish to have papers accepted for publication, to be awarded grants, or to be promoted, it is wise for them to conceal their political views."

This is otherwise known as a "chilling effect." When a group of people feels that their instincts or opinions put their livelihoods or good standing in danger, they repress them. The best option is to keep a low profile and hope to remain under the radar.

Right-wingers don't make their ideological opposites feel this way. They don't pressure political conformity among colleagues, friends, and even strangers. They don't act out when confronted with an opposing view.

That's liberals and Democrats. They don't like different opinions. They would rather not entertain them. It's too traumatizing.

Like a mental patient who sits peacefully until exposed to something nonsensically triggering, they snap at the sound of an edgy joke or a competing idea.

Try it and you're *canceled*!

CONCLUSION

Learning to Live with Liberals, Rule #1: Don't Feed the Animals

Imagine living in a perpetual state of heightened anxiety, anger, and sourness from the moment you wake up, until the second you fall asleep, each and every day. That's what it is to be a liberal Democrat anymore. It has to be said that not all liberals and democrats are anti-social, maladjusted, antagonistic individuals. There are plenty of nice ones! But if any given person is antisocial, maladjusted, and antagonistic, the data irrefutably show that he or she (or they/them) is almost certain to be a liberal Democrat.

And it's not that they're bad people. They're just so frequently in a bad mood that it sucks to be around them. It wouldn't be of dramatic concern if their overbearing gloom was a simple matter of choosing to tolerate it or distance yourself. But it's not. The misery felt and spread by modern liberals comes with severe consequences.

It means going through a once-in-a-century pandemic with mass death and trauma, accompanied by the ultimate nags who won't shut up about masks, staying home, and "social distancing." It did not matter that you lost your business and watched your hopes and dreams and everything you worked for dwindle away in a matter of days. There was no sympathy if you couldn't say goodbye to loved ones in the hospital or receive proper closure with a funeral. That wasn't forced on us by a pandemic. It was forced on us by bitter Democrats who told us that there was no reason we shouldn't be perfectly content shut in our homes streaming TV all day, so long as we got a government check.

That level of hysteria earned them tangible policy victories. They threw out voting regulations, scared everyone into giving up their freedom to congregate and travel, and flooded the country with more precious welfare money that caused yet more problems with inflation and supply and labor shortages.

And then they said every bit of the agony wasn't because of them, or because of an easily transmissible, airborne virus, but because of one man. A man who just so happened to be the person they were hoping to deny reelection.

Their misery might have made everyone uncomfortable but they got everything they wanted.

Liberals used their incessant fury to literally turn the 2020 election into a hostage situation—vote as they say or there would be more rioting, looting, violence, and vandalism. Everyone received the message. Residents of our biggest cities boarded up their shops and homes because Democrats had made clear that a certain kind of unrest, no matter how aggressive, was justified. Agitating mobs meant some people would die, but that was a price they were willing to pay in an election year.

A Democrat's emotional unbalance can be fatal in every sense of the word.

And the mistaken belief by independents and Right-wingers that these people would calm down after the 2020 election should have been well put to rest by now. What we've learned since is that there will be no end to the grief. It's here to stay.

Whatever it takes. They will rehash old wounds, use the weight of the federal government to persecute their enemies, and remind you each day that this is what you get for their trouble of having to look at you.

That's what the ongoing drama over January 6, an event that made up a fraction of the cost, time, and devastation that liberals wrought from 2016 to present day, is about. We will never hear the end of their PTSD stemming from a few thousand Trump supporters—white ones!—who opened a few congressional office drawers and broke a vase or two.

There is, however, an answer to all of it. We might be stuck coexisting in a country where half of the population is composed of excessively irritable, spiteful, and vicious people. But it doesn't have to run and thus ruin the country. It's not entitled to deference or acquiescence. Submission isn't the only option. It can be contained.

Admittedly, that's not easy. As noted, most non-Leftists prefer harmony over conflict, discretion over discord. It's easier. It's more pleasant. Confrontation can kill the day. But that's where some resolve is required on the part of everyone fed up with rioting, never-ending COVID restrictions, race baiting, and every other miserable thing liberals have rained down on America.

The wound can be cauterized in order to prevent more infection by first denying liberals and Democrats their demands. The demands have no limits. When they sense that their bullying scheme has had an effect, Democrats turn up the agony. The only way to ensure that they don't is to reject it from the start.

Unfortunately, liberals don't give up so easily. They've shown what they're willing to do to get what they want. There is no reason to believe that they won't recreate a year like 2020 if they have to. That's when things get more uncomfortable but not impossible. Liberals will call you a racist, a bigot, an "insurrectionist," a science denier. That's fine. The answer to that is you, and all of us, have families and livelihoods to protect and no one is going to take any of it away simply because liberals woke up on the bitchy side of the bed. They shouldn't get the keys to the kingdom each time they throw a fit.

Everyone has a right to defend what's his and do what's best for his family. That right has been placed in jeopardy by the joyless Left. It's not too late to save it.

ACKNOWLEDGMENTS

Documenting and explaining the bitchy nature of American liberals is about as fun as having a root canal without Novocain, but many people made writing this book immensely less painful than it might have been without them. Thanks to my publisher David Bernstein for giving me one more opportunity to put my thoughts down in another book; to my friends Michael and Nick for always offering the most thoughtful feedback; to my family for their unwavering support; and to Jordan for being so patient and great throughout me doing this in every single way.

ABOUT THE AUTHOR

Eddie Scarry is a nationally recognized journalist for the *Federalist*. He is based in Washington, D.C. and is frequently featured on Fox News and in the *New York Post*. Follow his latest commentary on Twitter @eScarry.

Made in the USA
Middletown, DE
30 June 2022

68079338R00086